TALES FROM THE ATTIC
PRACTICAL ADVICE ON PRESERVING
HEIRLOOMS AND COLLECTIBLES

TALES

PRACTICAL ADVICE

FROM

ON PRESERVING

THE

HEIRLOOMS AND COLLECTIBLES

ATTIC

COLLEEN WILSON

ROYAL
BRITISH
COLUMBIA
MUSEUM

Victoria, Canada

Published by the Royal British Columbia Museum,
675 Belleville Street, Victoria, British Columbia,
V8W 9W2, Canada.

Printed in Canada.
See page 120 for information on illustrations and production.

National Library of Canada Cataloguing in Publication Data
Wilson, Colleen.
  Tales from the attic

  ISBN 0-7726-4638-4

  1. Heirlooms – Conservation and restoration.
2. Collectibles – Conservation and restoration.
3. Preservation of materials. I. Royal British Columbia Museum.

NK1127.5.W54 2002   745.1'028'8 C2001-960262-6

Contents

Foreword

Conservation in the Museum

Museum conservators are a group of dedicated professionals who are responsible for the care of objects in the collections. Our major responsibility is to prevent the deterioration of artifacts.

Conservators gain specialized training from university conservation programs. We are taught to identify the materials in all kinds of artifacts and determine how these materials deteriorate, then how to prevent or slow down the deterioration. We are also taught techniques for conserving objects and to evaluate various conservation processes and methods.

By providing a safe haven for an artifact – stable relative humidity and temperature, proper light levels, and regular inspections for signs of deterioration – we can prolong its life considerably. Museum conservators regularly inspect objects for invasive insects, and treat them if necessary; we maintain safe light and humidity levels; and we advise exhibits staff on the best ways to display artifacts, often helping them with the job. Before an object is placed in a collection, we examine the storage method and type of packing materials to determine if they might damage the object they are meant to protect – the best storage material is inert.

If an object is in need of repair, conservators evaluate its condition and determine the best type of treatment, based on current research. Sometimes, treatment is straightforward and simple; at other times, it can be extremely complex, requiring weeks to analyse the material, research treatments and techniques, and undertake painstaking, detailed repairs.

Museum conservators train other museum staff how to safely handle artifacts and how to mount them for display in an exhibit. In every aspect of handling and storage, we treat all objects equally and individually, whether a rusty old saw blade or a rare watercolour.

Conservators-in-training are required to complete an internship in a recognized conservation laboratory. Our lab at the Royal B.C. Museum has helped train many students from throughout Canada, the U.S.A. and Europe. We openly share our knowledge and experience with interns, and much to our delight, we also learn from them about a variety of conservation principles, practices and treatments.

Royal B.C. Museum conservators respond to many public inquiries about caring for treasured objects in the home. It seems that spring-cleaning encourages many people to look at ways to preserve their heirlooms and collectibles. Answering similar questions from the public every year inspired one of our conservators to write articles on the most commonly asked questions. Colleen Wilson's "Conservator's Corner" became a regular column in *Discovery*, the news and events magazine of the Friends of the Royal B.C. Museum. Her bright and witty style made it one of *Discovery*'s most popular features.

In this book, we have compiled almost all of Colleen's articles, from Spring 1995 to Summer 2002; she has updated and expanded some of them. The first section deals with general enemies of conservation: dirt, light, humidity, bugs and what we like to call inherent vice – natural deterioration. The rest of the sections deal with specific kinds of objects, organized roughly by types of materials. Almost all of them cover the care and preservation of common family heirlooms and collectibles. A few cover subjects more specific to museums; they are included to give you some insight into the challenges faced by conservators and other museum staff. And you may find them useful in dealing with similar items in your home; for example, the article on First Nations poles may help you preserve a wooden bench or sculpture in your back yard.

Colleen does not try to answer all the questions you might have about heirlooms and collectibles in your home. (That would make an impossibly large book.) But you will find that she answers many, and that she relates the basic principles of conservation. Every object has a story. Fending off the agents of deterioration will help keep the story alive. But sometimes preserving the story means doing nothing: sometimes the best thing for an old artifact is to keep it in a safe place and just let it be.

Val Thorp
Chief Conservator
Royal B.C. Museum

A peek into
a typical museum
conservation lab
(Gerald Luxton, RBCM).

ADVICE·FROM·THE CONSER VATOR

Introduction

A Thing of Beauty is a Job Forever

I was introduced to the concept of entropy by a chemistry professor who described it like this: a car driving into a brick wall produces a pile of rubble, but a car driven into a pile of rubble will not produce a brick wall.

I have always thought of conservators as Anti-Entropy Forces – gallant and dedicated individuals valiantly trying to hold back the inevitable onslaught of chaos. (And as a textile conservator, I feel we should be wearing flowing capes.) It is not possible to make artifacts last *forever*, but we can try. It is possible to create an environment in which some things will endure for *a very long time*.

There are artifacts that are thousands of years old. In some cases they are all we know of their time and place. Material history tells its own story. It is not that I distrust words (or writers), but words change their import and they tend to be packed with opinion. Interpretation of the past is always coloured by the interpreter. The most objective and clear-headed historian is still influenced by her own culture, by the fashions of the day, by other writers on the subject. The costume designer for *Gone With The Wind* tried hard to make Scarlett O'Hara's dresses historically accurate, but looking at the movie now it is clear that the 1860s dresses were designed with a 1930s perspective. Artifacts never lie. They may be mute – or we may be deaf to them – but the information that they contain of their time and place is irrefutable. An 18th-century child's corset can tell us many things about tech-

11

nology, social patterns, hand skills, trade and commerce. But it doesn't make any judgements. It just is.

From such unadorned information we can learn. We can measure our successes and failures against the achievements of another time, we can draw inspiration from solutions that others have devised, we can rejoice in the continuity of human concerns, and in the individuality of our own lives. As we search for ways to improve ourselves, to improve the world, it is always useful to have examples of other ways of doing, other ways of living.

The conservators' job – our mission – is to make sure that this information is available as long as possible. We don't want to confuse matters with additions and we don't want to remove any potentially informative details. It is impossible to anticipate what information may be of interest in the future, or what analytical techniques may be available to extract it. Restorers make things look as if they were new again. Conservators try to look beyond the pretty face, try to maintain not only the appearance, but the inherent story that each artifact carries. The conservators (in their flowing capes) are standing between the car and the brick wall because they know that even if the pile of rubble could be reassembled, it would not be the same. It might look the same, but the details of placement, of mortar composition, of patterns of weathering would not be those of the unstruck wall.

This book of essays will enable you to participate in the conservators' mission. You, too, can feel that you are upholding Truth every time you turn out the lights; you, too, can make the world better for future generations by the use of a vacuum cleaner. But you have to provide your own cape.

ENEMIES & VICES

How Light and Light It Grows;
How Dark and Dark
Our Woes

Conservators are often accused of wanting to keep everyone in the dark. (Untrue!) Charged with the task of preserving artifacts forever, we battle our most potent enemy – light. While it cannot be eliminated from the museum's galleries altogether, in the interests of future generations, we try to reduce the destruction.

Light hurts! It fades the natural colours of fur, feathers, wood and basketry materials. It breaks down the delicate proteins of silk and the gelatin of photographs. It causes paper to turn brittle, rubber to crack and skin to split. Its effects are cumulative. A lighting level of 200 lux+ for one hour will damage as much as 100 lux for two hours or 50 lux for four hours. And the damage cannot be reversed. Once the dye has faded, the colour is gone forever.

This is why there are no windows in the museum's galleries – sunlight is too dangerous. Still, artificial light is

+ Lux is a unit of illumination equalling one lumen per square metre. An object that is a foot (30 cm) away from an average candle recieves 1 lux; an object five feet (1.5 metres) away from a standard 60-watt light bulb receives 50 lux.

not much better. Like the sun, most fluorescent tubes emit ultraviolet (UV) radiation. This high-energy radiation is ultra-destructive, yet is does not illuminate. UV radiation does not contribute to brightness, because its rays are invisible to our eyes. The windows of the museum foyer and any fluorescent tubes must be coated to filter out the UV rays.

Even so, visitors to the museum are not greeted in the foyer by displays of light-sensitive objects like weavings, butterflies and watercolour paintings. These items reside in the galleries, where we keep illumination to a kindly 50 lux – the internationally recognized standard for the illumination of sensitive materials. Not very bright, but as you move through the galleries, your eyes will become accustomed to less light and you'll find that it is enough to see fine detail.

At home, light reigns over preservation – a sunny room has much more appeal than curtain fabric. Precious possessions can be shielded from ultimate destruction by eliminating unnecessary illumination. If you are out all day, close the blinds and protect the carpet. Hang watercolours and needlework on north-facing walls or in an interior hallway. UV-filtering film can be applied to windows.

Destructive rays are a necessary evil if we are to see and enjoy any of the treasures from the collection. But for the conservator, the only place where the woeful burden is lifted is in the storage areas. There, the precious artifacts repose safe from change, wrapped in a protective layer of darkness.

Relatively Humid, Isn't It?

Warm air can hold more moisture than cold air – a cubic metre of air saturated with water vapour will hold 10 grams at 10°C, 30 grams at 30°C. The moisture in warm air will condense where the temperature drops, such as next to a cold window. Relative humidity (RH) is the percentage of moisture actually in the air compared to the maximum it could hold.

Organic materials contain water, and they love to conform to their surroundings. In a dry environment, wool tapestries, ivory and horn spoons will donate moisture to the atmosphere; in humid conditions they drink it up. A mask from the rainforest will have a different idea of a hot place than a saddlebag that has never been out of the desert.

Conditions of very high relative humidity can lead to mouldy oldies, particularly if there is inadequate air movement. Where moisture is abundant, insects are more active and chemical activity is accelerated. On the other hand, imbibing a little humidity can relax the elderly. Desiccated artifacts may be damaged by vibration or movement. If relative humidity is very low, organic materials will shrink, though not all will shrink at the same rate.

Outdoor humidity varies seasonally, but the relative humidity indoors changes whenever we adjust the thermostat. When the heat is turned up for human comfort, the available moisture drops for artifacts. For young and growing matter, these changes are a part of life. But dry old artifacts have a harder time responding to change. Most artifact material can accommodate a range of humidity levels, but those with parts under stress (canvas on a stretcher, skin on a drum) or composite materials (gilded or painted wood, inlaid furniture) risk damage in a fluctuating environment. Older, less flexible members of the family collection are most likely to be bent out of shape in a changing world. They can avoid damage if changes are slow and gradual (though they may never stop reminiscing about how much better the RH was in the old days).

Storing a skeleton? Choose a closet on an inside wall. The mass of material around it will moderate humidity changes. Packing or display cases that incorporate absorbent materials in their design can moderate humidity changes. If the case is reasonably well sealed, wood or silica gel will protect the contents from abrupt daily changes. One gram of silica gel per litre of air in the case is the most effective buffer. Put the gel into a moisture-permeable dust-defying container (a cotton bag is good). Store the gel in an area with the desired RH for at least two weeks before sealing it in the case with the artifact.

Things that go Chomp in the Night

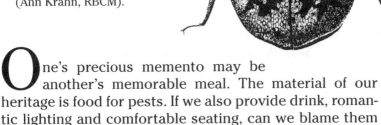

Adult Varied Carpet Beetle
(*Anthrenus verbasci*),
about 20 times actual size
(Ann Krahn, RBCM).

One's precious memento may be another's memorable meal. The material of our heritage is food for pests. If we also provide drink, romantic lighting and comfortable seating, can we blame them if they move in?

Moths fly to mind when we worry about heirloom consumption, and while the larvae of certain moths can devour a lot of historical evidence, other consumers are interested, too. Mould and fungus spores are happy to get together in a damp collection of books and papers. The larvae of carpet beetles, like those of the clothes moth, select vintage proteins – wool, fur, feathers, horsehair. Other beetles prefer to see wood, grains or garbage on the menu.

Our heritage may also be raw materials to non-consumers. A box of old love letters is potential bedding to amorous squirrels. Birds in the basement and bats in the attic find stored furniture attractive perches. Rats and mice would be happy to exercise their dentures on your old dental equipment. Household pets view antique carpets as wrestling partners, hanging textiles as playground equipment.

Adult Common Clothes Moth (*Tineola bisselliella*), about 3 times actual size (Ann Krahn, RBCM).

There are no quick and easy solutions. Mundane as it may seem, the best protection against pests is neither traps nor deterrent herbs, but good housekeeping. Carefully inspect the treasures you bring home: a trove of damp books that you've acquired at a garage sale could introduce silverfish to your library; a wool carpet from an estate sale could establish a lineage of clothes moths; carpet beetle adults can be carried in on garden flowers. Look for damage and sand-like droppings: these diners are not invisible. Block or screen holes and drains to discourage larger pests; eliminate sources of moisture so they will go elsewhere for a social drink. Keeping your collection areas tidy will remove some of the materials that attract pests, reduce the places they can hide and make any evidence of their visits more obvious.

Poisons just change the problem. The fragrance of a poisoned rodent is a banquet invitation for protein-hungry insects. And any chemical that will kill a pest can harm a human. Insect infestations can be terminated by a quick trip to the freezer. Forty-eight hours in a chest freezer will destroy all stages of any insect that is caught unawares. Bag artifacts in polyethylene to retain their original moisture content and provide a pest-free environment after freezing.

But the worst pest does not chomp at night. In the words of Pogo, "We have met the enemy and he is us." We make the decisions to allow the dogs on the furniture and postpone inspecting the attic, we handle our heritage with sticky fingers and wear historic clothing to costume parties. Precious heirlooms are not devoured by mysterious invisible forces. All the pests that are interested in your collections are visible; the difficulty lies in turning on the light.

Conservation Sucks!

When an artifact comes to the museum it may not be pretty, it may not be clean. Does that bother the conservators? *No!* We are Trained Professionals, we are Scientists. How do we treat the ugly, the broken, the dirty evidence of B.C.'s past? We don't.

Dirt is often what makes the artifact interesting. Soil and stains can tell us how or where an item was used. Boots with dried manure on them tell a different story than the same style of boots straight out of the box. In a social history museum, researchers try to look beyond the pretty face – a worn and stained set of children's long johns made down from an adult pair is as eloquent as a pristine party dress.

Cleaning can obliterate history. Erasing the doodling in an old textbook makes that book less personal. Washing a basket can remove the only evidence of what it carried. The paint stains on Emily Carr's smock set it apart from other smocks cut from the same pattern.

Conservators try to preserve the physical evidence of the artifact's history so it can tell its own story ... and continue to tell its story in the future, when analytical techniques have advanced and other pieces of the historical puzzle may come together. Conservators try hard not to add anything to the artifact, and we try hard not to subtract anything. That is why, although we are Trained Scientists, conservators *do not abhor a vacuum*.

The museum can be a dusty place, but not because it is full of old, dead things. Most dust is created by people. Carpet fibres are trampled and kicked into the air; skin flakes and falls; and hair, dandruff and lint all become dust. This is not a part of the artifact's history that warrants preservation. Conservators vacuum up the dust.

If the artifact is flat – like a map or a doily – we place a screen over it before vacuuming. For three-dimensional artifacts, we wrap a net over the vacuum nozzle so beads or feathers are not sucked up. We use a soft brush to sweep the dust toward the suction.

Like many good housekeepers, conservators try to avoid in the first place. Artifacts are displayed in cases where possible, or stored in individual containers draped with tissue or cotton dust-covers. But if dust does creep in, we conservators are poised, ready to defy Nature and up the suction.

Damned Artifacts

Creators do not always sub-scribe to the Gospel of Conservation. There are those who believe that cultural materials are part of the timeless cycle of decay and rebirth. There are those who believe that planned obsolescence is part of a critical cycle of manufacture and retail. Some close their eyes and think of entropy. Conservators look over their shoulders and whisper, "Inherent Vice." An evil lurks in the hearts of some artifacts that conservators are powerless to exorcise: many things are not designed to last.

Fashion is rarely tempted by immortality. Shoddy goods, incompatible materials and mechanical stress are inconsequential once styles change. Items that will soon be discarded because they are "out of date" need not be well planned or constructed. Parasols, party shoes, com-puters – no one cares what condition they will be in after 10 years.

This is not a new attitude. One hundred and fifty years ago, inferior silks were given more body and scroop (the high-pitched sound when silk is compressed) by adding metallic salts. By the turn of the last century, *weighted* silks could be up to 400 times their original weight. The cost savings must have been as impressive as the rustle: weighted silks were used extensively for coat linings, wedding dresses and petticoat flounces. Unfortunately, the combination of silk and tin is chemically unstable. No amount of conservation research has found salvation for these fragmenting fabrics.

French Ivory was once considered more versatile than ivory and bone; rubberized cloth required less care than leather; pressure-sensitive tapes are more convenient than glue and paper. But new is not necessarily better. Now, French Ivory is oozing nitric acid, rubberized cloth is turning sticky, and tape is turning yellow and staining paper. The road to artifact hell is paved with spray coatings, quick fixes and E-Z care products.

Great though the rejoicing might be for the salvation of any precious heirloom, it is important to recognize the limits of redemption. Newsprint, for example, is made for news, not olds. Paper conservators are tormented by the eternal burn of acidic wood-pulp newspaper clippings. Those precious birth announcements and festival highlights would last longer if photocopied onto acid-free paper.

Sometimes it is difficult to distinguish between an incompatible combination of materials and compatible materials in an environment bent on their destruction – it is worthwhile to seek a conservator's judgement. Wasting limited resources on damned artifacts is the devil's work, indeed.

Genius at Work

Leonardo da Vinci is renowned as a scientist, artist and inventor. He is less well-known as a Friend of Conservators.

Leonardo da Vinci created *masterpieces*, works that the world wants preserved. *The Last Supper* has provided employment for conservators for hundreds of years. Instead of using a fresco technique with a 300-year-old pedigree, Leonardo *invented*. He used a new method and experimental materials, and worked in an unstable environment. The stream running under the wall provided a constant source of moisture – a great facilitator of chemical change. The only other thing he could have done to sweeten conservators' pension plans would have been to install skylights.

Leonardo was a creative person, not content with tradition. Conservators are, well, *conservative*. They want things to remain unchanged. The materials and techniques that conservators use are rigorously tested, but it is difficult to determine what will last forever. Despite ingenious accelerated-aging trials, many materials that are here today may be gone tomorrow.

The best proof of long-term stability is a history of longevity. Materials that have remained unchanged for the past 500 years are more likely to survive the next 500.

Environments that have promoted preservation for the past 1,000 years are a good bet for the next millennium. Experimenting with the wisdom of the ages can be risky if you want to leave a historic legacy. It is expensive to keep propping up something that was unsteady in the first place.

You may be an artist; perhaps you are a genius. But when inspiration strikes, remember the future. If you have produced genuine *cultural icons*, conservators may curse your unprepared ground, your unstable pigments, your experiments with adhesives and sealants, but they will be glad of the employment.

If you feel your work may have to stand up to the centuries on its own, however, you should be looking at the tried and true. You may think such a conservative attitude might hamper your creativity. But if you achieve a beautiful watercolour sky, only to find in 20 years that it looks green because the paper has yellowed, you may reconsider the economy of using non-rag paper. When your gorgeous, hand-woven tapestry becomes slimy along the edges, you may regret the quick paint-on solution for fraying yarns.

For a lasting opus, seasoned wood, washed fabric and primed canvas are as important as inspiration.

HARD & FAST

Hi-Yo Silver,
Tarnish Away!

There are few things more elegant than fine silver, but what can be done about tarnish now that the butler is gone?

Tarnish occurs when silver reacts with sulphur, forming silver sulphide. Sulphur is present in our environment in many forms – it is released by foods (egg yolks, Brussels sprouts, mayonnaise), natural rubber (rubber bands, latex gloves), textiles (wool, felt) and paints.

Sulphur is also part of the gaseous pollution resulting from burning coal, gasoline and wood. The rate of tarnishing increases in humid conditions, and the chlorides in salt will accelerate the reaction further. The damp ocean air of British Columbia's coast is perfect for tarnishing silver.

All methods of removing tarnish remove some of the silver as well. It is important to choose a polish that will neither scratch the surface unnecessarily nor remove too much of the silver. Excessive cleaning with an abrasive will wear away incised decoration and obliterate hallmarks; removal of too much silver from electroplate will reveal the base metal. The active ingredient in silver dips is a strong acid that quickly removes tarnish ... and silver; they also contain a suspected carcinogen, thiourea. Galvanic cleaning using aluminum and washing-soda can

29

strip the silver from electroplate and leave silver dull, lustreless and much more susceptible to re-tarnishing.

But there is hope for your tarnished silverware. Conservation scientists have identified Twinkle Anti-Tarnish Silver Polish as suitable for heavily tarnished silver. For maintaining a polished surface, they recommend Hagerty Silver Gloves with R-22, and Birks' Anti-Tarnish Silver Polishing Cloth. These gentle polishes also provide protection against future tarnishing. But products can vary and formulas may change, so consult a conservator for the most recent recommendations.

If silver is to be kept in storage it will keep its shine longer if it is protected from sulphur in the atmosphere. Wrap it in acid-free non-buffered tissue or an anti-tarnish silver tissue, and seal it in a polyethylene bag.

When you are handling silver, try to avoid skin contact. The acids in your skin will etch your fingerprints into the silver. Of course, you could wear white cotton gloves – the butler would certainly approve.

All that Glisters is not Gold

Ormolu, spelter, silver gilt or pinchbeck. Our fascination with metals that dazzle like gold is not new.

Pure gold is unchangeable – tarnish will not darken it, nor corrosion wear it away. But gold is too soft to use on its own, and it has always been expensive. Making candlesticks and clock cases out of something hard (and cheap) then coating it with gold reduces the cost, increases the lustre and eliminates the need for constant repolishing.

Sounds brilliant, doesn't it?

The problems arise because the cheaper materials underneath are not immune to corrosion, the gold layer is very thin and the bond between the two metals is sometimes not very strong.

From fool's gold to tinsel Lurex, there is much that glisters. Silver gilt is silver coated with gold – often seen inside sugar basins. If the gold wears away, the silver will darken with tarnish. Sometimes silver leaf is coated with a tinted varnish, both to protect it from tarnishing pollutants and to colour it gold. Ormolu, which is brass or bronze with a thin coating of gold, was used for decorative objects such as clock cases. However, just as ormolu is an imitation of solid gold, there is also an imitation

31

ormolu – bronze dipped in acid to give it a gold colour, then lacquered to prevent tarnishing. Spelter has a base of a lead-zinc alloy with a gilt surface. It is brittle, liable to damage and the gilt is not well attached. Pinchbeck is a copper alloy similar to brass. It was sometimes gilded, and because its colour is similar to gold, it may be hard to see when the gold has worn away until the base metal tarnishes.

If you feel like "going for the gold", go easily. Regilding is unwise, as the colour of modern plating is quite different and will certainly compromise the original appearance – if not the value – of any antique. Cleaning can damage poorly attached gilt, and water can get into hollow areas of a casting and accelerate corrosion. Synthetic detergents may contain sulphur, which will stain exposed silver. Because the gold layer is so thin, even handling can wear it away. Polishing will not add any lustre to real gold and can remove a lacquer that preserves a good imitation; polish left in joints or decorations can attract moisture.

Twenty-four carat or electroplate – if you have a heart of gold, dusting with a soft brush is the safest method to keep it gleaming.

You Deserve a Medal!

Trying to preserve things means fighting the most inexorable enemy of all: change. Just keeping a shine on your medals calls for attention above and beyond the call of everyday collecting.

Medals that muster together become scratched and abraded. Even tiny nicks and pocks interfere with light reflection; they also make the surface more difficult to polish effectively. Each medal should have its own container.

The metals of medals want to get out there and skirmish with undesirables – acids, chlorides and sulphides. These are easy to encounter. They lurk in sweat, paper, unfinished wood, vinyl, salt air, wool and wood smoke. Tarnish is the result.

To defeat this action, give your medals the white-glove treatment. Jettison your vinyl pockets and invest in acid-free paper folders and boxes. Consider polyethylene or polypropylene photographic pages for storage and display.

Tarnish is not the enemy, but it brings out the enemy within *us*. Valorous acts of polishing can wear the surface away. While most military medals have a bright surface, some, such as the Victoria Cross, were issued patinated. Some also have painted or enamelled decorations. The patina on commemorative medals from fairs and congresses and on military medals can be valuable. Polish only those that were originally bright. A jeweller's cloth is suitable for removing light tarnish on silver or brass medals. A dip cleaner applied with a swab may be useful for heavier tarnishing. Avoid submerging medals because dip cleaner can over-clean the recesses in the design. Rinse well with water after any cleaning.

To prevent further change, waxing is preferable to lacquering. Degrease the medal in a well-ventilated area by soaking it for several minutes in alcohol or acetone. Mix equal parts of good-quality paste floor wax and mineral spirits (e.g., Varsol or Shellsol), and apply with a soft cloth, using a warm hair dryer to melt the wax into recesses. If tarnish reappears, the wax can be removed by soaking the medal in mineral spirits.

If your medals are flanked by ribbons, the campaign becomes more complicated. Pollutants that create tarnish on metal will also weaken and discolour fibres – isolation is the only defence. The ribbon is an important part of any medal, but polishing will endanger the fabric. Detach and label, so the two can be reunited once the waxing is complete. While metal is not injured by overexposure to light, fabric is. If your medals hang on ribbons, try to march on the shady side of the parade. Light levels of more than 50 lux[+] (enough to see the "whites of their eyes") will cause dyes to fade and ribbon fibres to part company.

[+] See footnote on page 15.

Not a Farewell to Arms

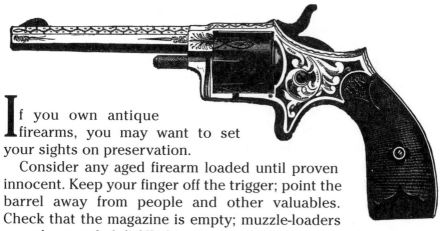

If you own antique firearms, you may want to set your sights on preservation.

Consider any aged firearm loaded until proven innocent. Keep your finger off the trigger; point the barrel away from people and other valuables. Check that the magazine is empty; muzzle-loaders were frequently left filled, sometimes with more than one charge. Gunpowder can remain explosive for a hundred years or more. Mark the interior length of the bore on a dowel and compare it to the exterior of the barrel. If the mark is shorter than the touch-hole or nipple base by 3 cm or more, there is a charge or obstruction in the barrel. Consult a conservator or gunsmith.

Although capable of great destruction, firearms are composite artifacts sensitive to both environmental and mechanical stresses. The acids and salts on your skin can etch fingerprints into polished metal. Even if you have no need to conceal evidence, wear white cotton gloves. Arrest corrosion by limiting exposure to acids and excess humidity. Unfinished particleboard, plywood, mahogany, oak and most adhesives give off acidic vapours that can accelerate rusting and tarnishing. Leather scabbards and cases are also very acidic. When stored, firearms will benefit from being wrapped in acid-free tissue. Cover display mounts with a neutral material such as unbleached cotton. It is safest to use two hands when lifting your aged arm, as the stock may be weak or split. Never "dry fire" an antique firearm – cocking can break the mainspring; pulling the trigger can snap metal.

If you feel that cleaning is necessary, remember that tool marks and wear – the patina of use – are part of an artifact's history. Remove caked-on dirt, wax and dried polish with a wooden scraper – metal tools can scratch. Light rust can be removed with a nylon scrubbing pad or 0000 steel wool rubbed lightly in the direction of tool marks. But do not use an abrasive on steel that is mottled blue, brown or grey, as this is an original finish. Dark-green patina on brass is stable and desirable; bright-green verdigris is not✛. The latter can be removed with a wooden scraper or pick, then swabbed with mineral spirits. If brass should be bright, try a little polish-impregnated wadding (e.g., Duraglit) wrapped around a toothpick end. Do not overpolish; metal corrosion may hide information that could be removed by overly vigorous cleaning.

Unless you are a gunsmith, do not break down your ancient weapon for cleaning. Firearms were designed to enable hunters and soldiers to do basic maintenance, but no more. Most have a unique assembly, and disassembly must be documented with drawings and photographs, the parts laid out in order. The person most likely to be able to re-assemble a firearm is the one who took it apart.

Clean gunmetal was traditionally oiled. Polish off the excess with a soft cloth, or dust will stick and the adjacent material become stained. The original finish on wooden components should also be preserved. If the firearm is to be handled frequently, consider applying a thin coating of microcrystalline wax.

The Canadian Firearms Act★ designates as antique most arms manufactured before 1898 that have not been

---

✛ A patina is a film that forms with age and can be charming; but verdigris is a rust that can damage brass or copper.

★ Call 1-800-731-4000 or consult www.cfc-ccaf.gc.ca regarding the Canadian Firearms Act.

redesigned. There are special rules for some handguns manufactured before 1946 that allow them to be handed down within a family; reproductions may qualify if they are of black-powder models. Antique firearms do not need to be registered, nor do you require a licence to buy, sell or give them away. If you aim to preserve firearms, target information first.

Gems of Advice

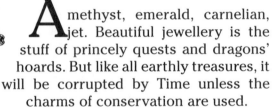

Amethyst, emerald, carnelian, jet. Beautiful jewellery is the stuff of princely quests and dragons' hoards. But like all earthly treasures, it will be corrupted by Time unless the charms of conservation are used.

Storing your jewellery in a dragon's cave has some advantages: security is great and light levels are low. Turquoise, topaz and lapis lazuli can change colour or fade, and opals can fracture if exposed to prolonged sunlight. Ultraviolet radiation can cause white zircon to revert to brown. On the other hand, in the heat of a dragon's fiery breath, amethysts may change colour, and garnets and sapphires crack.

Having pirates bury your treasure will avoid both light and heat, but it is difficult to control humidity on the Spanish Main. Marcasite is sensitive to high humidity, and aquamarines can crack in water. Steel beads will rust. And with all that heave ho-ing, jewels can be damaged by abrasion. Diamonds can scratch other diamonds. Tiny scratches on the surface of a polished gem or metal setting reduces reflectiveness. Rubies, emeralds, sapphires and topaz can be fractured by sudden knocks and shiv-ering timbers.

Jewellery is best stored in individual containers. It may come in a specially designed box, but remember that the acids in ordinary cardboard, felt and leather cause silver to tarnish. Pouches of cotton or linen are ideal for rings and brooches, but necklaces and bracelets should be rolled in acid-free tissue to prevent abrasion and tangling. Necklaces should be kept straight to reduce strain on the string. Avoid contact with cotton batting or polyester bat-ting, whose fibres can catch and pull. Attach any labels with thread; adhesives can harm metals.

If you are going to flaunt your finery, inspect it first with a magnifying glass. Ensure that all mechanisms – links, clasps, hinges – are sound. Old gold is softer than modern, and links can wear through easily. Consider a safety chain for valuable necklaces, bracelets and brooches. When dressing for the ball, don your jewels *after* applying scent and hairspray. Amber and pearls are sensitive to solvents, and the blue dye that changes jasper to Swiss Lapis can wear off in the presence of cos-metics and perfume. Like Cinderella, don't wear your opals while defrosting the freezer, and take off your gold rings before working in the garden.

Before any attempt at cleaning your jewellery, make sure all stones are secure. Work over a towel-covered tray in case anything falls. If the setting is open (back of the jewel exposed) and the piece does *not* include pearls, opals, ivory, enamel or turquoise, it can be cleaned with a little neutral detergent in warm water. Apply the solu-tion with a stencil brush✜, rinse in clean water and leave to dry on tissue (drying with a cloth could snag the claws). With enclosed settings, moisture can damage the foil at the back. Freshen with a dry stencil brush or wipe with a swab dampened with isopropyl alcohol. Pearls, opals and turquoise can be drycleaned with powdered magnesium carbonate. Place the jewel in a plastic jar and

---

✜ A stencil brush has short, stiff bristles projecting from a circular tip. It's used to dab paint or ink through a stencil plate.

cover with the powder. Shake gently, then leave overnight. Remove powder traces with a soft brush.

Whether your jewels were mined by evil trolls or purchased from a reputable dealer, a little extra care will ensure that they are still worth a king's ransom.

Bead-Decked
and Bead-Dazzled

T he star of many an ensemble is the decorative bead. Giving weight, colour, swing and glitter to garments and furnishings, these tiny performers have been made of almost every imaginable material, from porcelain to papier mâché to plastic. But any attempt at preservation must take the supporting cast into consideration.

Although some beads are collected as loose items, most are strung, sewn, knit or wired to another material. Sometimes the expectations placed on the backstage crew are unreasonable. Individual beads do not weigh very much, but a beaded dress or bag can be much heavier than the foundation fabric can sustain. Find a box or tray to house each item; using it for storage and transportation will reduce potentially damaging handling. Store garments flat and gently stuff bags and cushions with acid-free tissue to retain their shape.

A Sekani First Nations beaded bag in the collection of the Royal B.C. Museum (RBCM 2913 V.6).

Reduced handling will also mean less soiling. Although even sawdust can be vacuumed off beadwork using a soft brush and a net over the vacuum nozzle, greasepaint and sweat are more difficult to remove. Even small amounts of water can dissolve pigments on decorated beads and aggravate potential "glass disease". The thread holding the bead will absorb the soiled water and become weaker or carry soil into the supporting fabric. In some cases, it is possible to clean beadwork with swabs barely dampened with fast-drying ethanol (ethyl alcohol). The effect should be tried in an inconspicuous area first and the swabs changed frequently.

Some beads may appear more stage-struck than others. Glass that was incorrectly manufactured can suffer from glass disease. Beads that appear to be sweating or have a crusty deposit, beadwork that has bleached its image onto the supporting fabric or produced a darkened image on leather – these beads may be breaking down. Cleaning with ethanol can slow down this deterioration if the item is subsequently stored in a consistently dry environment. Silica gel can be used to maintain 45 to 50 per cent relative humidity in a closed container. Steel beads, too, will appreciate these dry conditions.

When beads are in the spotlight, remember that light can be harmful. Beads of organic materials, such as wood, seeds or rolled beetle wings, will fade and degrade. Except for polyester, all threads holding the beads are also susceptible to light damage.

It is rarely possible to match the colour and size of old beads, and it is impossible to guess at missing design elements. Beadwork is sometimes dated by its most recent beads, so modern replacements can mislead collectors. Loose beads can be secured by stitching through the last few beads on a strand, though where the supporting cast is frail, additional backing may be required. A carrying tray will act as a safety net – if the worst occurs and beads are dropped, those caught can be counted upon to perform again.

The Genie in the Bottle

Y ou're out beach-combing and something in the sand catches your eye. An old bottle! What a find! But before you start to polish it....

Sometimes a bottle that has been buried looks quite ordinary at first, but as it dries, colours appear mysteriously. This magic is deterioration and is caused by a chemical imbalance in the original manufacture. Handling (and certainly polishing) can cause the iridescent layers to come off in flakes. Water will accelerate the deterioration, so keep this bottle dry and don't handle it.

In advanced stages of deterioration, iridescent glass may weep or sweat and may develop cracks or crizzles✛. This is sick glass that cannot be cured. A sealed storage container enclosing silica gel to keep the relative humidity below 42 per cent is all that can protect this glass from its own evil nature.

If your bottle was in salt water and appears to be flaking as it dries, throw it back. Re-submerge it in salt water

---

✛ A crizzle is a defect in glass. Crizzles form a network of fine cracks inside the glass, resulting in a loss of transparency.

and gradually (over days) introduce fresh water. Once all the salt is removed, the bottle can be stored in 70 per cent ethanol. If it dries out, this bottle will self-destruct.

But perhaps there is no iridescence, no crizzling, no flaking. Sound bottles can be cleaned by soaking for two to three hours in Calgon, borax or a biological washing-powder. Bottles with labels should only be wiped after protecting the label with plastic wrap. The interior can be cleaned by filling, rather than soaking. Use a bottle-brush to dislodge unwelcome spirits. The smell of perfume can be removed with alcohol, though it may take more than one hour-long soak to effect the disenchantment. A jammed stopper can be loosened with WD-40, but be sure to dry the interior thoroughly before replacing it; a piece of tissue paper will prevent the stopper from jamming again.

Take care in removing any stopper, and think twice about cleaning out the contents. If the bottle is closed, it could contain interesting clues about its use or history. Cloudiness inside the bottle could be a lime deposit associated with deterioration, impossible to remove without damaging the glass. Then again, it could be the smoke of a genie, swirling angrily inside.

Plastics Forever?

The plastic handle of this 1920s purse was in excellent condition when it was collected by the Royal B.C. Museum in 1976 (RBCM).

By 1996, the handle had cracked and oozed almost beyond recognition, and caused some corrosion of purses stored nearby (John Veillette, RBCM).

Although we think of them as products of this century, plastics have been with us since the 1830s. They seem impervious and indestructible, filling up garbage dumps with no intention of breaking down. Many people fear they will be with us forever. During the 19th century, modern alchemists strove to turn cheap cellulose✛, from wood pulp and cotton waste, into materials imitating silk, ivory and tortoise-shell. Reacted with nitric acid, cellulose forms cellulose nitrate (nitrocellulose), which, combined with camphor, produces celluloid. Patented in 1869, celluloid was used as photographic film and as a moulded

---

✛ Cellulose is a carbohydrate found in the walls of plant cells; it is the main structural material of plants. Paper and plant-based textiles, such as cotton, consist largely of cellulose.

plastic. It became fashionable in the early 1900s, marketed as French Ivory or Ivaleur. Moulded celluloid was used for dresser sets, lamps, clocks, picture frames, manicure sets and an extensive line of fashion accessories.

Unfortunately, cellulose nitrate is extremely flammable. And despite our belief in the immutability of plastics, celluloid slowly breaks down as the cellulose becomes denitrated. Even more unfortunately, as the nitrates break away, the tendency to burst into flames increases. This has become a serious concern in collections of photographs and motion picture films.

Because moulded celluloid was not nitrated to the same degree as film celluloid, it is not likely to ignite spontaneously. But its breakdown is no less destructive. Once deterioration passes a certain point, the plastic quickly yellows, shrinks, becomes brittle and turns into bad-smelling fragments or foam. Nearby materials can be reduced to powder by the strong acids released by the plastic meltdown.

Impurities in the original cellulose or in the processing may account for the deterioration of some pieces of celluloid, while others of the same vintage remain pristine. We know that high temperatures, light, pollution, physical stress and high humidity will accelerate the deterioration, but there does not, as yet, appear to be any way to stop it. For the time being, the best thing to do is keep celluloid artifacts isolated. But make sure they are well ventilated or they will only make themselves worse stewing in their own acidic juices. Placing them in a freezer should slow down the chemical reaction, but this is expensive for museums and, perhaps, impractical for collectors.

Given what we know about these materials, we have reason to believe that other types of plastic will also self-destruct eventually. The material history of the 20th century will bear little resemblance to life as we lived it if there are no plastics in the museum collections of the future.

Uneasy Pieces

There was no hope for Humpty Dumpty – but things might have been different had he been ceramic. Should your precious ceramic dish or ornament have a great fall, wrap the pieces individually in tissue; if the shards grind together, they will never fit perfectly.

It is important to determine the type of ceramic. Earthenware has been fired at a low temperature and is reddish in colour. Stoneware, fired at a higher temperature, is heavy and the body (the unglazed portion at the bottom) is usually white or grey. Porcelain, the hardest and most glass-like, has been fired at the highest temperature and is thin, fine, even translucent.

Before putting your ceramic together again, make sure it is clean and free of grease. High-fired ceramics can be soaked in water and detergent. Fragile earthenware should merely be dusted with a soft brush. A dishwasher is unsuitable, even for intact ceramics, as it can remove decorations such as overglazing and gold edging.

Clean, dry ceramics can be glued. Polyvinyl acetate (ordinary white glue) is best for earthenware and stoneware that are not intended to hold water. For other stoneware and porcelain, a clear epoxy (such as Sun Cure) is best. Unless the join is very simple, choose an epoxy that has a longer setting time than five minutes to enable you to arrange all the shards.

A practice run using self-adhering tape can determine the best order of re-assembly. If there are many fragments, fit the base together first. Sometimes a group of small pieces can be assembled before joining them to the larger shards.

Spread glue on both sides of the join and clamp the pieces together. Use a box of clean sand to position the ceramic together so that the join is balanced. You can also mould a support out of Plasticine. Remove any excess glue after the join is secure but before the glue has completely hardened.

Proceed slowly. Mix a little epoxy at a time – it is better to secure one part and return later to attach the next. Otherwise you will be wishing you had all the king's men (though probably not the horses) to help hold all the pieces in place.

A shattered high-fired ceramic plate can be repaired ...
if the pieces are assembled with care and patience (RBCM).

SOFT & EASY

An Ounce of Prevention
A Recipe for Leather Care

French Polish for Boots and Shoes
Mix together two pints of the best vinegar and one pint of soft water. Stir into it a quarter of a pound of glue, broken up, half a pound of logwood chips, a quarter of an ounce of finely powdered indigo, a quarter of an ounce of the best soft soap and a quarter of an ounce of isinglass✛. Boil for 10 minutes or more. Then strain the liquid and bottle and cork it. When cold, it is fit for use.

– *Enquire Within Upon Everything* (83rd rev. ed., Houlston & Sons, London, 1891)

Is *this* how to care for leather – those expensive trousers, your exquisite upholstery, valuable book covers, or precious baby shoes? Research on the care of aged leather has shown that traditional treatments, French polish and saddle soap among them, have major drawbacks.

Dressings are not useful. Oil-based dressings can attract pests and accumulate dust. They can also soften original finishes and decorations, and actually stiffen the leather as the oils oxidize with age. Water-based dressings, while softening oils and soils, usually drive them

---

✛ Isinglass is a clarifying agent made from the membranes of the swim bladder of certain fish – a standard ingredient in kitchens at the time.

53

deeper into the skin. Very fine, light-coloured leathers may have been tawed⁺ rather than tanned, and can be irreversibly damaged by water. Historic leathers can be more difficult to conserve and have less research value if modern dressings have been applied. Repeated applications of saddle soap will make aged leather stiffer, just as too much washing will dry out your skin.

Instead of searching for that pound of isinglass, try an ounce of prevention. Protect your valuable leather treasures from soil – from dust and dirty hands – and protect them from pollution. The cheering blaze in the fireplace of your library of leather-bound volumes will produce sulphur dioxide, which can speed up deterioration and cause irreversible red rot★. And don't draw that favourite leather armchair up to the fire, either. New skin will

Leather items from the Royal B.C. Museum collection (Jim Fielding, RBCM).

⁺ Tawing produces a thin, soft leather that was used for things like babies' hats and ladies' gloves. It was treated with alum and salt rather than tannins.

★ Sulphur dioxide combined with airborne moisture can form sulphuric acid, which breaks down collagen fibres in leather. As deterioration progresses, the leather becomes red. In advanced stages, the leather turns to powder.

shrink and become brittle at 60-75°C, but aged leather can be damaged by even lower temperatures.

Fluctuating humidity levels will result in a progressive hardening of vegetable-tanned leather. Too much moisture can also cause problems; leather shoes stored in a damp cellar will soon sport mould and mildew. But bringing them out into the sunshine will expose them to other dangers. Sunlight will fade, dry and shrink leather; it will also accelerate the action of pollutants and the oxidation of dressings. Leather, once the protective skin of some animal, requires the same shelter from the sun that our own skin requires. Tanning is no protection against looking like an old boot.

Fur Futures

As the weather warms and fur-bearing animals leave their dens, we humans prepare our furs for their summer hibernation.

Fur and cold seem to go together. Since the 1890s, cold storage has been used to slow down the insect pests that eat fur. Humidity controls ensure that the skins are neither too dry (and crack) nor too moist (and support mildew).

Sending furs to cold storage is not a necessity, however. As a mammal with a second-hand coat, you might want to take care of your fur yourself.

For a healthy, glossy appearance, fur needs to be groomed. Brush it with a soft brush toward the screen-covered hose of a vacuum cleaner. But if it is soiled, don't lick it clean – older pelts may have been treated with arsenic or DDT to discourage insects. Try cleaning it with cornmeal: warm the cornmeal in the oven and work it through the fur, then remove it thoroughly with a brush and vacuum cleaner.

Unfortunately, nothing can prevent hair loss. A live mink grows new hair; a mink stole, never. As the skin ages, the hairs will eventually loosen and drop out. The type of animal to whom the skin originally belonged and the method of processing the pelt will affect when the hair will be shed, but nothing can reverse the inevitability of balding.

To eliminate insect problems, use the freezer. Refrigeration will immobilize insects, but a quick plunge to -20°C will kill them at any stage of life. Pad the sleeves and folds of the garment with tissue or nylon net to prevent the skin from being damaged on sharp folds. Wrap the garment gently in tissue or a washed cotton sheet to protect it from direct contact with moisture condensing on the inside of the bag when the garment thaws. Seal the garment in a large plastic bag, remove excess air and leave it in a chest freezer for 48 hours. On removing the fur from the freezer, allow it to thaw completely before opening the bag.

If you leave the bag closed, though, you can squirrel it away in the back of your den until the change of season leads you to start stockpiling food and putting on those extra layers. You can frisk about all summer knowing that you have provided a climate-controlled, pest-free, micro-environment for your winter wrap.

Something Old,
Something New,
Something Borrowed,
Something Blue

Walking down the aisle in an heirloom wedding gown can seem like a special way of continuing a tradition. Unfortunately, unless great care is taken, this can reduce the chances of the gown surviving for future generations to appreciate.

An antique gown can look unique, often because it was made-to-measure with fine hand-sewing. While it is obvious that a garment cut to fit one person may not fit another, with historic fashions there are additional complications. Until the 1920s, women wore corsets and their dresses were cut accordingly. To achieve the flapper look of the '20s, many women wore flatteners. In the 1950s, women wore restricting girdles and highly structured brassieres. Fitting into a dress from another period of fashion can be tricky, and wearing a dress that does not fit correctly can put excessive strain on both fabric and construction.

While marriage is supposed to last forever, wedding dresses were not always created with longevity in mind.

Dresses made with fabric that can only be dry-cleaned often have decorations that will dissolve in dry-cleaning solvent; dresses made with fabric that is best wet-cleaned may be lined with material that will shrink in water. Older wedding gowns are sometimes impossible to clean.

If you do decide to wear your family heirloom, some additional care will help protect it. Ensure that it fits without strain. Use an under-dress to protect aged fabric from contact with your skin. Wear dress shields instead of using a deodorant; the salts in perspiration and the chemicals in antiperspirants can damage fabrics. For the same reason, do not wear perfumes and be very careful with cosmetics. Consider changing into something less vulnerable after the photographs have been taken – a smear of lipstick or a spilled drink can cause irreparable damage.

If current dress styles do not appeal to you, there are many patterns available for reproducing the fashions of other times. A dress cut to fit you in the lines that you choose will enable you to preserve your family treasure and create something special to pass on to your daughter. You can always wear the family jewels.

This is the Way
We Wash the Clothes

When it's early Monday morning and there are aged textiles in the laundry, there is a bit of a song and dance to do before we actually wash the clothes.

This is the way we rate the water. Hard water contains mineral ions that can form a bond between soil and fabric. Water must be soft, or washing will not be effective. Unfiltered tap water may contain impurities that can be deposited on fabrics. Filtering will remove particulates, but distillation is necessary to remove minerals. Even gentle washing is agitating for aged textiles; it should be done in clean water, or not at all.

This is the way we choose a detergent. The cleaning action of soap is dependent on its alkalinity and is much greater in hot water. Some detergents can perform in cooler temperatures and neutral conditions. Unfortunately, most commercial detergents contain dyes to make them look cleaner, perfumes to make them smell fresher and optical brighteners to reflect ultraviolet light, making your laundry appear "whiter than white". These additives are intended for laundry that will be washed over and over again; left as residues on heirlooms that are washed once and put away, they can cause yellowing and fading. Just because the package says the detergent is suitable for delicate textiles, doesn't mean it is safe for cleaning antiques. Look for soap whose main ingredient is sodium lauryl sulphate, a gentle cleaning agent that is used in shampoos for farm animals (but not flea shampoos) and other mild detergents.

This is the way we assess the fibres and structure. Cottons and linens can stand high temperatures and the alkalinity of soaps. Wools will felt✝ if exposed to heat, alkalinity and agitation; silks maintain their lustre best in cool water and neutral conditions. Layering or padding may contain dye or soil that can surface unexpectedly. Some combinations of fabrics can preclude washing altogether – if its cotton lining shrinks, the silk vest will be ruined.

This is the way we test the dyes. Place a few drops of washing solution on each colour and blot them. Choose inconspicuous locations such as seam allowances or loose threads on the back of the fabric, but make sure to test every colour, including those used in repairs, trim and additions. If any colour runs, test all of them again with a little vinegar in water and failing that, a little ammonia in water. Some unstable dyes can be controlled by altering the pH of the final rinse – once dry, a bled dye is irreversible. While many old wives used salt to set dyes, it remains in the fabric, creating complications in the long term.

This is the way we remove the stains. In general, it is impossible to remove old unidentifiable stains. Spot treatments can weaken fibres, leaving a hole instead of a stain. Bleaches based on chlorine are far too harsh for

---

✝ When you've mistakenly put a wool sweater through the hot cycle and it now fits the dog, you've felted it – matted the fibres and shrunk the structure.

aged fabrics. Formulas are available for gentler bleaching, but are only suitable for undyed, undecorated cottons and linens.

Even the gentlest of hand washing is very hard on old textiles. Water, detergent and structure must all be compatible. If not, it is time to plant another mulberry bush. Washing is out of the question.

Lady Macbeth
Visits the Drycleaners

Out damned spot!
out, I say!

If a little water will not rid your treasured textile of its spots and stains, you might consider drycleaning. Solvents can clean effectively without causing shrinkage or loss of dyes. Drycleaners have a wide range of solvents and specialized equipment for stain removal. It is important to remember, however, that the drycleaner's business is keeping contemporary clothing looking new, and that's not always suitable for fragile heirlooms.

Because the solvents used for cleaning are health hazards, cleaning and drying are done in an enclosed system, like a washer and dryer. Because the solvents are an environmental hazard, they are re-used. Soils and dyes in old solvent occasionally re-deposit on fresh loads.

63

Even in the hands of an expert, the removal of old stains is not straightforward. It is often difficult to identify the stain, and after years of interaction with the fabric, it may not respond to gentle treatment.

Many old garments have dressings unfamiliar to modern cleaners. Laces and trims were sometimes stiffened with milk or sugar water. Sugar cannot be removed by solvent cleaning, and the heat of the dryer can caramelize it, turning the lace dark brown. (The same thing can happen with forgotten spills of colourless soft drinks.) Drycleaners will remove any plastic trims and accessories before cleaning, because some plastics will dissolve in solvent cleaners. If your garment contains plastic, you may want to reconsider drycleaning, because the original construction cannot be retained. Drycleaning strips the synthetic dressings that are present on new fabrics. In order preserve that new feel, replacement dressings are routinely added. These are fine for garments that will be drycleaned repeatedly, but we do not know their long-term effect on aged fabric.

Most soil is not harmful. We have been taught that cleanliness is not only next to godliness, but essential for happiness and critical for preservation. The physical agitation of drycleaning can do more harm to an aged textile than most soils. Many stains are so ingrained that their removal weakens the fabric. Most drycleaners are willing to discuss your concerns. But before considering cleaning of any kind, know whether you would rather have an intact but soiled heirloom, or a clean one with holes. Consider whether you want to preserve the buttons on the wedding dress or Grandma's stitches holding them together for tomorrow and tomorrow and tomorrow.

A Warning Against Old Quilts for Warming

As the days become darker and colder, it's time to look for something to keep us warm.

A quilt is a cosy thing, designed for snuggling. But before you decide to put Great-Aunt Grace's nine-patch on the couch ... does anyone like to snooze there? put their feet up? snack? Greasy hands and grubby feet can put your quilt in hot water. And although soil is not generally harmful to old textiles, cleaning is. While many quilts were created with laundering in mind, many that have been passed down were "best quilts", too special to be worn out through everyday use and cleaning.

If you are thinking about washing an old quilt, it is essential to check the colour-fastness of every fabric used. Unless there has been damage, though, it is difficult to know what has been used inside. Mosaic patches in the English tradition were worked over pieces of card or paper, which were sometimes left in place. Utility quilts were sometimes padded with old blankets or clothing that may not be clean or colour-fast. Because a quilt can be extremely heavy and prone to damage when wet, it can be difficult to rinse adequately. On drying, soil from the interior can rise to stain the surface.

Preserving an old quilt means not getting it dirty in the first place. Let Great-Aunt Grace's handiwork warm your eyes instead. Displayed on a spare bed, it can be enjoyed – but removed when guests start yawning. Remember that if your spare room is sunny, the quilt on the bed will fade faster than the one in storage. And a quilt on a wall will fade faster still if brightly or continuously illuminated. A hanging quilt can also be soiled if hung in a dust-collecting location, such as over a heater, or within reach of pets or children.

If the colours and design of a quilt are kept bright, the memory and respect for the quilter will long warm our hearts. In these dark winter days, as we consider the fabrics of our own lives, old quilts can be a hotbed of inspiration. Rather than snuggling under that old quilt, put on another sweater and fire up the sewing machine.

The Magic of Carpets

Abeautiful carpet can transform a hovel into a residence of rare delight, but this spell can be easily broken.

Enchanting as its appearance may be, the carpet has a simple structure: a woven backing with tufts of pile. The tufts of wool or silk or rag carry the design, but the backing is critical. If damaged, there is nothing to prevent the design from flying away.

The first Oriental carpets to reach Europe were valued so highly they were used on tables rather than floors. If you prefer not to walk on art, you may wish to hang your precious rugs on a wall: a hook-and-loop fastener (e.g., Velcro) sewn to the top edge will give uniform support. Choose a location without direct sunlight to avoid fading.

Carpets on the floor are also subject to damage from light, as well as abrasion and soil. An underlay will cushion the backing, but greater traffic – in an entranceway, in front of a fireplace – will expose the pile to more wear. A carpet you value is unlikely to retain its charm under a dining table.

Surface soil and dust can be spirited away with a vacuum cleaner. Lift the carpet occasionally to remove the fine grit that has sifted through. More extensive cleaning can be problematic. If the backing is soaked in the course of wet-cleaning, it may not dry quickly. Damp backing is prone to mildew and may damage the floor. Do-it-yourself rug-shampoo units use very little water, but inadequate rinsing can leave detergent in the carpet, and future soil will cling to the sticky residue. Steam-cleaning is designed to refresh modern hard-wearing carpets. Like any cleaning done in place, it will clean just the surface – anything deeper would put the backing and floor at risk.

Working absorbent cleaning material into the pile to be vacuumed away later reduces the risk of damaging the backing, but can leave behind debris that will attract insects. Although many carpets can be safely hand-washed in soft water, there is risk for both the pile and backing. With rugs made in countries where water is not abundant, dyes may not have been adequately rinsed and can later run in washing. If the backing material is weak, such as the burlap of rag rugs, just the weight of water

can break its yarns. A wet carpet should be dried quickly and thoroughly – easier said than done when you are dealing with something dripping, heavy and liable to be damaged if sent flying through the air.

For protecting your carpets from moths and carpet beetles, no spell works as well as good housekeeping. Inspect carpets frequently; check underneath for frass (gritty insect droppings) and signs of damage. Moth larvae can move between the carpet and floor, sheering off the pile without disturbing the visible surface. Wrap infested carpets in polyethylene and whisk them into a chest freezer for 48 hours.

Roll carpets with the pile out to protect the backing. For long-term storage, wrap them in plastic sheeting to protect them from insects and moisture. Like a genie in a bottle, a carpet in storage does not need to breathe. Choose a dark, dry location and the magic will still be there, even after a thousand and one nights.

A Stitch in Time

A n old sampler, a piece of colourful Berlin wool-work, a cross-stitch commemorating the birth of a child – all are stitches suspended in time. Mounting and displaying such needlework can not only keep that distant moment before our eyes, but can provide timely protection from soil and damage.

Adhesives, though quick and easy for mounting work, yellow with time and become stiff and intractable. A piece of needlework merits a sewn support.

Fome-cor (a sandwich of Styrofoam and acid-free card) provides a lightweight, chemically stable backing that can be cut with a utility knife. If you already have a frame, the Fome-cor should fit loosely – you will not be able to adjust it later. Choose a firmly woven backing fabric. For a sampler or hemmed needlework, this backing fabric may be visible and should complement the piece. For canvas work or needlepoint, unbleached cotton is a good choice. Wash and rinse the fabric thoroughly.

Cover one face of the Fome-cor with the fabric, pinning around the edges to align the grain and keep the tension even. Turn the Fome-cor over, and glue the edges of the backing fabric to the back of the Fome-cor. Use either

69

white glue or hot-melt glue, and leave a 1.5 cm (0.5 in) glue-free margin around the edge.

When the glue is thoroughly dry, pin the needlework to the front of the backing fabric. Sew the needlework in place, trying to stitch between the threads. Make the stitches snug but not tight – a curved needle may be useful. Make extra stitches around heavy decorations, loose fragments and damaged areas.

Framing protects by sealing out soil, pests and pollution, so it is important to use unbuffered, acid-free materials (see Problems with Paper, page 79). Use a mat or spacer bar to prevent the glass from touching the needlework.

Whether it is a treasured heirloom, your child's first embroidery project or the product of your own skilled hands, careful mounting will help to ensure that these stitches will be enjoyed for years to come.

Body Building Without Steroids

Allan Patten, RBCM.

What could be more indicative of social change than the clothing people have worn? From corsets to spandex, from silks to polyester, the garments we wear (and those we wouldn't be caught dead in) reflect changes in technology and changes in society.

When displaying historic garments (and this could mean last year's tree-planting outfit), conservators aim to support the fabric. Hanging out for ten years or more can put a real strain on our material history. The original wearers of vintage clothing were rarely fashion plates, so shop mannequins with their exaggerated features and postures are not suitable. To support the clothing completely, a museum mannequin must replicate the body that originally wore the clothing.

But like body builders everywhere, conservators must avoid banned substances. Acids from wood and paper products, solvents from contact adhesives and paints can react with the artifacts we are trying to preserve. Unstable plastics can release fumes that are hazardous to mount and artifact alike. The bodies conservators build are designed to *last*.

Trying old clothes on even a perfectly sculpted body is wearing on the clothes. To reduce handling, we measure all aspects of the garment, including the circumference of the interior, at 5-cm (2-inch) intervals. Then we cut discs of 5-cm Styrofoam, corresponding to the circumference measurements, and stack them on a backbone of dowels. Working from stacked discs wastes less Styrofoam than carving from a solid block. It also gives the conservator-sculptor a general shape from which to start and helps keep the form symmetrical. The dowels keep the discs aligned and reduce the need for adhesives. Styrofoam (polystyrene) is a stable material – unless exposed to ultra-violet light – and is readily available and easy to carve. Once the form is smooth, we build up any deficiencies with polyester batting and then cover the whole body with batting to maintain a soft surface. Finally, we give the entire mannequin a body-suit of cotton-polyester jersey.

We make no attempt to articulate these perfect bodies. Even giving them heads could detract from the clothing they support. They embody postures and figures that are no more. Come to our exhibit galleries and reminisce. You probably won't even notice the mannequins as you recall double-knits and sequins. Look back and see that although our bodies change, our clothing can last forever.

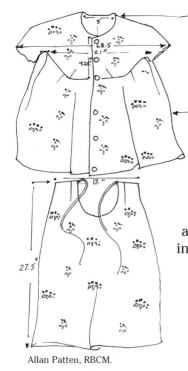

Allan Patten, RBCM.

WORDS & PICTURES

Dirty Books

Some people can't wait to get their hands on a dirty book. In their excitement, they forget to wash their hands; they forget to put on white gloves. Without stopping to remove the dust, they flop open the book covers. The dust falls inside. They flip through the pages. Notes and cards fall to the floor. Now they have dirty postcards, too!

The books we treasure range from the rare first edition to the well-thumbed reference. A little care will ensure that they will endure to tempt the bookworms of the future.

Pressed flowers in your gardening books will let soil sift between the pages. Instead, put the flowers in a labelled envelope of acid-free paper and place a paper in the book noting where the envelope is stored. Make your notes in pencil – don't stain the pages or covers with ink that can smudge or run.

But don't let the marginalia in that old Latin text bother you. Pencil marks of previous bibliophiles provide clues to a book's history. Really disfiguring marks can be removed if the paper is not coloured and is in good condition. Using a soft eraser, work in straight lines from the spine to the edge of the page. Stop if fibres begin to pull from the surface. Coffee, tea, ink, oil and the stains left by self-adhering tapes are extremely difficult to remove and require the advice of a professional conservator.

If your nautical books get flooded, stand them on end, fan the pages open and dry them as quickly as possible. If there are too many to deal with at once, freeze them, defrosting batches after your other problems dry out. Don't dry wet leather or parchment bindings until you have tapped your conservation advice sources.

The presence of silverfish is a clue that you have hidden your mystery books in too damp a location. Excessive moisture can soften binding adhesives and cause warping and cockling. Shelved against an outside wall, in an unheated room or basement, damp books can develop brown spots known as foxing. They can also grow mould. To remove the spores and smell of mildew, ventilate the book thoroughly without direct heat or sunlight. When completely dry, brush and vacuum, taking care not to recirculate the mould spores.

Silverfish
(*Lepisma saccharina*),
about 4 times actual size.

When pages begin to fall from your family tree, resist the urge to tape. Self-adhering tape will damage both paper and binding before becoming brittle and ineffective. Document-repair tape can be used if the book is merely old, not treasured – but use it on only one side of the paper. Loose pages and covers can be held in place with soft cotton ties. Very fragile books are best protected in acid-free boxes.

The next time you go to the source for that half-remembered quote, take a soft brush, or better still, your vacuum cleaner. Keep the book firmly closed and, with the spine up, gently brush the dust away. If you're not using the vacuum, step outside the library to brush it, or dust will just settle on the next enticing volume.

Advice for Bookworms

Bookworms have long striven to preserve their collections, but too often the joy of acquisition and the desire to read has strained their legacy.

The medieval codex was made of very stable materials: parchment, wood and vegetable-tanned leather. Even the most ardent bookworm owned very few of them. There was room to store *Sir Gawain and the Green Worm* horizontally. But rare is the bookworm who can set limits. As collections increased, collectors began to store books upright. When vertical, the block of pages is shorter than the cover boards and weighs down the top of the binding. Eager bookworms also grab the top of the spine to pull the book from the shelf, adding to the strain.

With the advent of printing, shelves became crowded; the embossed leather of *Wormeo and Juliet* rubbed the gold from *The Merry Worms of Windsor*. Opening wide the only known copy of Aristophanes' *The Worms* put such stress on the joints that the boards fell off.

As bookworms increased the demand, things went from bad to worse. Binding construction deteriorated, and by the 19th century the quality of materials had declined. Paper made from wood pulp is cheap but contains acids that result in dry and brittle pages. Cardboard is lighter than wood, but is more susceptible to damage. Fabric covers are more fragile than leather. The 20th century saw even more books in the hands of even more bookworms. Classics like *Little Wormen* and *For Worm the Bell Tolls* were carried in pockets, propped beside dinner plates and left open face down on beach towels. And with the industrial age came increasing pollution. The *Origin of Species* may have changed the world, but the world also changed the book. Sulphur dioxide from automobile exhaust and factory smoke reacts with vegetable-tanned leathers, causing irreversible red rot[+].

It is time for the worm to turn, get your nose out of that book.

Book shoe

Position bookshelves out of direct sunlight and away from sources of excessive heat and moisture. Keep the volumes absolutely vertical, but avoid crowding. Use book boxes of acid-free card to protect fragile volumes, both ancient texts and acidic paperbacks. Book shoes also protect the sides and support the text block, while leaving the spine visible. When removing any book from the shelf, reach behind and push until the sides can be firmly grasped.

Handle your books as the treasures they are – where will you ever find another copy of *The Rub'aiyat of Wormar Khayam*? Open new books carefully. Smooth down a few pages at the front of the volume, then a few at the back. Alternate until the middle is reached. A book rest with a gap for the spine will further protect the binding. If boards are loose, use cotton ties to keep them in place; all parts are valuable, even the dust jackets. You know that first edition of *Wormy Potter* will be a joy to bookworms yet unhatched.

+ See footnote ★ on page 54.

Problems with Paper

Are your prints powdering? photographs fading? documents discolouring?

Precious treasures are often mounted on cardboard, wrapped in tissue, stored in boxes. But paper products can harm the objects we hope to protect.

Most paper is made of cellulose extracted from wood pulp by strong chemicals. These papers contain acids left over from the pulping process and those that build up as the lignin✢ in the wood pulp breaks down. Sulphuric acid can also form through contact with sulphur dioxide and moisture in the air – the same phenomenon as acid rain. These acids break down the paper in a slow burn that can also scorch our treasured documents, discolour aged photographs, weaken delicate silks.

To preserve museum collections, we use acid-free papers. Paper can be made from cellulose that does not contain lignin, and without employing acids. Cotton and

---

✢ Lignin is a complex organic substance present in the cell walls of many plants making them rigid and woody.

linen waste are used to produce high-quality all-rag papers. While these provide a much safer environment for heirlooms, they are still susceptible to sulphur dioxide in the air.

To deal with this problem, alkaline-reserve (or buffered) papers were developed. But, unfortunately, these papers do not solve the problem: organic materials are very sensitive to alkalinity. Wool, silk, leather book bindings, and protein films on photographs and negatives can all be harmed if stored in buffered paper.

A recent development in archival materials, Micro-Chamber papers, incorporate activated charcoal. They claim to trap and neutralize contaminates in storage enclosures. Although conservators are cautious in recommending new miracle solutions, MicroChamber papers do look promising for extending the longevity of stored collections.

Acid-free card for matting and mounting is available at most art supply stores. Unbuffered acid-free tissue and boxes in many sizes are available from conservation suppliers, as are MicroChamber papers.

Fan-tastic!

Fascinated by fans? Unfortunately, these frou-frous of fashion were not fabricated to function for longer than a flirtatious flutter. Even when crafted of the finest materials by fastidious fanatics, the flimsiness of silver foil, of silk gauze and ivory filigree, and the different responses of paper and ivory, silk and wood, feathers and mother-of-pearl to their environment make fans among the most fragile of artifacts.

The frequency with which your fans are fondled will foretell their future. Flouncing and fluttering are fraught with peril for the fragile sticks. Folding and unfolding will forfeit the integrity of the leaf – flaking paint and split silk will follow.

Keep your fan flared, preferably on a mount faithful to its curves and slopes. A functional support can be formed of Fome-cor (see page 69) – large enough to accommodate the fan fully open – and wedges of polyethylene foam. Measure the height and length of the upper guard stick and cut a wedge of ¼-inch foam. Using hot-melt glue, attach it to the Fome-cor base. Take the height of the guard stick at the base of the leaf, and the length of the arc of the lower edge of the leaf. Glued to the Fome-cor at a right angle to the first wedge, the second wedge should

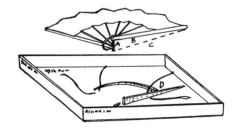

support each rib midway along its length so that it does not flex. Fasten the two guard sticks with ribbon ties to forestall strain on the leaf.

Feature your mounted fan behind glass to keep it free from dust and the subsequent friction of cleaning. Framed fans can look fabulous, but be fussy about your display location – too much light will cause colours to fade and fibres to fracture. For storage, add sides to the Fome-cor base so the fan trays can be stacked. Store your mounted fans in a dark, moderate and unchanging environment and the future will find you free to fandango with frequency.

If your fans are flecked with fluff, vacuum cleaning is the fairest method of refurbishing. Cover the vacuum nozzle with nylon net and, using a soft brush, flick the dust toward the suction. Grubbiness on paper fans can sometimes be gently removed with a little powdered eraser, followed by vacuuming, but practise on the reverse first. Ivory, bone or pearl sticks can be wiped with a barely dampened swab, but any further cleaning would be a fiasco.

Fixing something as flimsy as a fan can be very finicky. Although it may seem a fast and facile solution, forgo the use of tape. The adhesive will fail with time, leaving only a flagrant stain to mark your folly.

If all else fails and your frippery is looking frazzled, consult your faithful conservator.

You Have to Draw the Line Somewhere

Blithely scribbled or meticulously laboured, drawings can hold reality fluttering on the page. But they may not hold it there for long. The longevity of your favourite sketch is dependent on how it was made and how it is treated.

Aspiring artists have reached for paper and pencil for centuries, but papers vary. Those that contain acids will discolour and turn brittle. The small brown *fox spots* on old paper are a result of mould spores incorporated when the paper was made, but there are mould spores in the air all the time just waiting. Paper stored in a damp place is a perfect place for them to grow. Drawings hanging on a cold, outside wall can trap condensation – use spacers behind the frame to encourage air circulation.

Pencil is a very stable drawing medium. The pigments that give colour to charcoal and chalks are stable in light, but unfortunately, they can be easily smudged. Pastels powder as easily as chalk, but some colours are susceptible to fading. Crayons use the same pigments bound in a fatty material and are slightly stickier (even if the artist is older than five years). Although artists have experimented with fixatives over the years, collectors should refrain from using them. Modern fixatives may change the colour of some pigments and can seal in dirt. Put these drawings behind glass, not acrylic – particles are light enough to be lifted by the static electricity acrylic inspires. Hang them on a wall free from vibration – a slamming door or rattling furnace can shake those fine lines free.

In many cultures, over many centuries, lines have been drawn in enduring carbon-based inks. Not all inks, however, are sooty black. In the 20th century, artists drew on an increasing pool of colours. But the inks in fountain, ball-point and felt-tipped pens are dyes rather than pigments, and are very susceptible to fading. Crisp cartoons drawn with modern blue-black ink will soon become a mellow brown. Some of the colours used in felt pens will fade even in the dark; exposed to light they will be lost completely.

Old ink is not necessarily better, though. Iron-based inks were used widely in Europe until the early 20th century. Made with gallic acid extracted from oak galls, the ink destroys the paper beneath the line. These drawings are extremely fragile – and attempts to de-acidify them can be disastrous. Consult a professional conservator before you draw your own conclusions.

Old-master drawings made on rag paper or well-cured animal skins still capture our imagination. Before glass became inexpensive, they were kept in folders, protected from the damaging effects of light and pollution. With the advent of pulp paper, neon colours and fridge magnets, the works of many a young master will live to inspire a much smaller circle of admirers.

Does your Monet Need A Mop?

'Tis Spring, and we turn to fancy thoughts of ... cleaning. But as we take up mop and duster, we'll sweep right past the gallery.

Paintings on canvas are works in four layers: the canvas held taut on a wooden framework; the ground, a layer of chalk or pigment in glue or drying oil to stabilize the canvas and provide a smooth, non-absorbent surface; the paints, pigments in a binding medium such as egg, linseed oil or acrylic emulsion; and, on most though not all, a varnish coating to protect the paint and clarify the colours.

Many points in this structure are as weak as a housemaid's knee. The canvas and wood respond to humidity in different ways, creating destructive tension. The canvas is vulnerable to punctures and vibration. Any alteration of the canvas puts strain on the ground and paint layers. Pigments change under bright light, as can mediums if exposed to heat; varnish can yellow and darken with time. And Grime has no respect for Art.

If the painting has either sentimental or monetary value, only the lightest of dusting with the softest of sable

85

brushes is safe. The threads of a dust-cloth can catch edges of paint; a feather duster can scratch. Any kind of liquid cleaner can penetrate through microscopic fissures in the paint, dampening the ground or canvas, ultimately causing the paint layers to lift and flake. If darkened varnish and layers of soil are obscuring the artist's original colours, consult a professional conservator. (In less than professional hands, cleanliness can be next to gaudiness.)

Instead of reaching for the scouring pad, find some coreplast (plastic cardboard) and a screwdriver. A backing board attached to the stretcher will mitigate environmental change and vibration while protecting the canvas from punctures, debris and harmful labels. The backing should overlap the stretcher (but not the canvas) by 2 to 4 cm – for large paintings, cut the backing panels to correspond to the partitions created by the crossbars. Use foam strips on the stretcher for a good seal, air holes will produce localized environmental conditions. Use that elbow grease to tighten #5 non-corrosive screws and washers at intervals of 10 to 25 cm (4 to 10 in.). Although not traditional, installing oil paintings behind glass provides the greatest protection. Modifications to the frame may be necessary to ensure that the glass does not touch the painting.

Backing in place, brush off your hands and roll up your sleeves – now it is time to move some furniture. A painting over a fireplace or radiator will experience severe temperature changes and accumulations of soil. Choose an inside wall that receives indirect light in a room without tropical potted plants (misting is not good for paintings). Use general lighting – spotlights and lamps that mount on the frame concentrate heat and light on a small area of the painting. If your housekeeping plans necessitate storing paintings, find an area of stable environment (no damp basements or hot attics). Use sheets of cardboard to protect the frames and keep them separate.

Ac-Cent-Tchu-Ate the Positive✢

Holiday snaps, baby pictures, wedding photographs – these are positive ways to preserve your memories. But you'll need more than faith to ensure that pandemonium does not spread among your family photo files.

Rough handling can damage the surface of photographs; fingerprints can stain them. When you latch on to the affirmative, hold it carefully by the edges. Use a soft 2B pencil to label the back along the margin, as ink can bleed into the picture. Better still, label the folder.

Individual photographs can be protected in acid-free paper enclosures. Ordinary paper envelopes, including those from the photo-finisher, will deteriorate, damaging the contents.

If you prefer to put your prints in an album, maximum protection means polyethylene or polypropylene pages – both Vue-All and Print File make pocket pages to fit slides and several sizes of photographs; some have pockets for

✢ With acknowledgement to songwriter Johnny Mercer.

paper labels. The next best choice is an acid-free paper album, using Pigma pens for labelling – you can purchase these from archival and some photographic suppliers. All glues, as well as self-adhering tapes, have the potential to damage. To bring glue down to a minimum, attach photographs with Mylar photo corners – it's the only really safe way. If you buy pages separately, choose a suitable binder. Conventional binders are made of acidic card covered with vinyl (polyvinyl chloride), which breaks down, releasing acidic fumes. "Magnetic" photo albums, with their acidic card, pressure adhesive and vinyl covers, are extremely unstable.

But while you accentuate the positives, *don't* eliminate the negatives. They can be used to replace faded, stained or damaged prints. There are pocket pages for negatives, and for the past two years developers have used sleeves made of stable plastic. Make copies of photographic prints on display and slides that are frequently used – wear out the duplicates rather than the originals.

Store your photographs where the temperature and humidity don't reach the maximum. Heat will increase the rate of chemical deterioration; moisture will cause images to fade and the plastic of negatives and slides to degrade.

Regular colour prints will fade, even if they are kept in the dark. You may notice fading on some colour prints within two years; after fifty years, probably all will show some colour change. Instant colour prints are even less stable. For photographs that will outlive your memory, ask for black-and-white prints to be *processed for permanence*, printed on fibre-based paper. These photographs will last for centuries, but they will cost more and you will have to find a custom lab to do the work. If you want to leave a photographic legacy, you can't mess with Mr In-Between.

Not on Your Tintype!

Hand-tinted ambrotype and case (RBCM 976.96.32).

W hoa, Nellie, what's this we've found? A photograph in a tiny, folded frame. Tarnation, but it looks old.

Louis Daguerre hit pay dirt in 1839. The first successful photographs consisted of a sheet of copper coated with silver. Exposure to iodine, light and mercury fumes created a daguerreotype – an image in metal that can appear positive or negative depending on the angle of observation.

Daguerreotypes were so danged expensive that some bright spark up-and-invented the ambrotype. A sheet of glass coated with wet collodion✝ produced a negative image when exposed to light. Backed with black paper, fabric or paint, it appears positive.

But if you hankered to send your likeness to the folks back home, the ferrotype or tintype solved the problem. A sheet of iron was painted black or dark brown, coated with wet collodion and exposed. The image appeared positive against the dark background. Tintypes were

---

✝ Cellulose nitrate in alcohol and ether.

used from the late 1850s to the early years of the 20th century, and can be easily identified with a magnet.

While many a westerner was right proud to mail a tintype in a decorative cardboard mat, any of these types of photographs may be found in hinged cases. Union cases were moulded *composition*✢; others were made of wood covered in leather, pressed paper or fabric. Inside the case, the photograph sits in a recess in a brass protective binder that holds a sandwich of cover glass, decorative mat, image-bearing plate and, for some ambrotypes, a black backing.

Despite its fancy doodads, the case can be as fragile as the photograph. Handle these artifacts with cotton gloves – these photographs are very sensitive to pollution, and both case and photograph can be easily abraded. Leather hinges may be feeble from excessive use; wooden sides may become unglued; thin brass can be damaged by manipulation. While these photographs are not as sensitive to light as those printed on paper, many were hand tinted. Both pigments and case materials can fade. Moisture can play the dickens with both photographs and cases. Store cased photographs flat in conditions of constant humidity – a closed polyethylene or acrylic box is good insurance against disaster.

Dag nab it, you say, there's already moisture inside the case. The appearance of tiny droplets inside the cover glass may be a sign that the glass is deteriorating. This is a serious condition – hightail it to a professional conservator immediately.

But in most cases, this is a very stable package – disturbing something that has lasted this long is just asking for trouble; breaking any kind of a seal will reduce the value considerably. Daguerreotypes, ambrotypes and tintypes are photographic positives: there are no negatives from which to make additional prints. Like all artifacts, they are unique. A fine how-de-do from the past.

✢ A thermoplastic made of shellac, sawdust and pigment.

You Must Remember This

*In any man who dies,
there dies with him
his first snow and kiss
and fight....*

Ah, but the Russian poet Yevgeny Yevtushenko wrote before the advent of home videotaping. Now, not only the first snow, but the first storm and date and experience with Krazy Glue can be passed on. Unfortunately, magnetic tape is a fragile medium for bearing the weight of a lifetime of memories. Even if properly cared for, it may only last a few decades.

Videotape has three principal components: magnetic particles that store information, a polyurethane binder that holds the particles and a polyester tape support. Memory loss occurs when any one of these fails. The particles are affected by magnetic fields produced by electrical appliances, power tools and TV sets. Polyurethane reacts with moisture, becoming soft and sticky. The polyester base can be deformed by stress or high temperatures. Dropouts – white spots, flashes, streaks in the image – mean that some part of the tape is deteriorating.

If you are filming the birth of your first child, start with new high-quality tape. If you anticipate reliving this moment on every birthday, avoid using a longer-playing tape (such as T-160) – its polyester base is thinner.

Before you film the juggler tossing flaming brands to your partner, wind the tape from one hub to the other and back again to reduce the tension. Record at standard speed (SP). Rewind the tape after recording and every playback.

Those images of you in plaid bell-bottoms are now a part of history. Even if the memory makes you shudder, take care not to drop the cassette that holds it. Be sure to keep your video player clean and well maintained. Tape can be etched by minute particles. The priceless picture of the cat eating the wedding cake could be destroyed by dust, food or cigarette smoke. Use a dust-cover.

Don't leave a tape in the player overnight, or stop in the middle of a tape either – the longer you pause on your poetic triumph in the pie-eating contest, the sooner the picture will be gone. Insert and eject at blank sections of a tape only. After enjoying the hairstyles from an old family reunion, return the tape to a labelled plastic container. Cardboard provides little protection. Store the tapes upright – horizontal stacking can cause distortion.

Like babies in bubble bath, videotape should not be exposed to high temperatures or direct sunlight. Storing steamy images on a windowsill, in a hot attic or in a damp basement will break down the binder, deform the tape and encourage mildew growth.

Tapes that are more than ten years old and have been poorly handled and stored may now be no more reliable than our own memories. Deteriorating tape can be reformatted – re-recorded onto new stock. But have another look at that first snowboard ride with sideburns – maybe some images should be left to die.

ODDS & ENDS

Gather Ye Rosebuds While Ye May

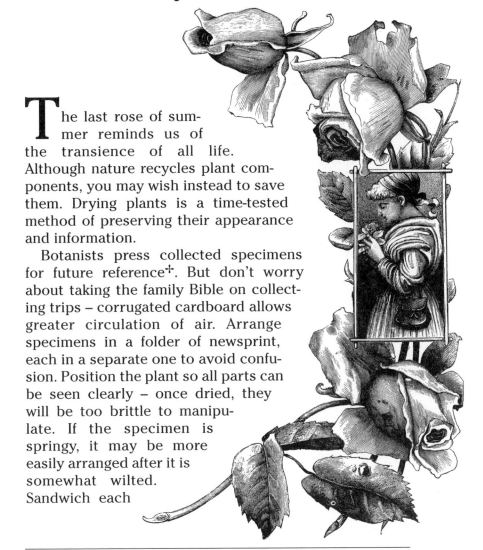

The last rose of summer reminds us of the transience of all life. Although nature recycles plant components, you may wish instead to save them. Drying plants is a time-tested method of preserving their appearance and information.

Botanists press collected specimens for future reference[+]. But don't worry about taking the family Bible on collecting trips – corrugated cardboard allows greater circulation of air. Arrange specimens in a folder of newsprint, each in a separate one to avoid confusion. Position the plant so all parts can be seen clearly – once dried, they will be too brittle to manipulate. If the specimen is springy, it may be more easily arranged after it is somewhat wilted. Sandwich each

---

[+] Budding botanists can find more information about preserving plant specimens in the Royal B.C. Museum book *Plant Collecting for the Amateur* by T. Christopher Brayshaw.

The plant press: newspaper, carboard, foam and press-backs ready to be bound with straps (T.C. Brayshaw, RBCM).

folder between layers of cardboard. For thicker specimens, thin foam or paper towels against one side will allow all parts of the plant to be pressed evenly. Place the stack of sandwiches between rigid press-backs, and strap or tie firmly.

The rose from your engagement is not well suited to pressing. While a tight bud may keep its shape, most three-dimensional blooms require support. Garden flowers or foliage of a stiff construction can be dried suspended upside-down. Softer blossoms retain their shape best if dried in silica. Ordinary fine sand, if thoroughly washed to remove all its clay, can also work as a desiccant. Nestle the specimen in a small bowl and gently pour enough silica or sand around the petals to cover the flower completely.

Whether dried flat or in the round, plants retain their colour best if they are dried quickly. Collect on a dry day – the more moisture the plant contains, the longer it takes to dry. Provide good air circulation. Gentle heat – over a stove or in a microwave – can facilitate desiccation. Remember to align the corrugations of the plant press to allow air to circulate through them. Check the press daily to remove any fully dried specimens and to replace damp paper towels.

Although flowers are created to attract insects, you will not want to preserve this relationship. Carefully inspect new specimens. If pests are found among your dried plants, place all suspicious material in a plastic bag and freeze for 48 hours.

Dried plants can be mounted on acid-free card with a little white glue. Herbarium specimens are glued or held in place by tiny bridges of paper. Keep the mounts in a folder or behind glass; they are too fragile for frequent dusting. And as much as roses like sunshine, your dried bouquet will fade if displayed in strong light.

Once dried, plant material can last for a very long time. To be of more than seasonal interest, however, information must be preserved with it. Without the location and date of collection, reference specimens are of no use. Sentimental collections benefit from well-kept records, too. Long after our autumn has faded into winter, documentation on the back of a framed bouquet can allow sweet memories to bloom anew.

The Care and Feeding of Baskets

Baskets have been storage containers, carrying bags and souvenirs. As works of beauty and skill, they are worthy of our care. But fibres that once held a stem up to the light, lived in the sun or gripped the earth – even though transformed by skilled hands – cannot forget their roots.

Made of plant material, baskets are sensitive to the world around them. Basketry fibres will break down and decorative patterns will fade if baskets are kept in direct sunlight. Baskets also respond to humidity. Too little moisture in the air will make the fibres brittle; too much moisture encourages mould and mildew. Too many changes in humidity can weaken materials under tension. Baskets will retain their strength longest if kept where there are no extremes of humidity.

Although once living plants, basketry materials no longer require feedings. Oils and varnishes not only alter the original surface, but can become sticky and difficult to remove. Baskets kept in the kitchen can also acquire a film of grease to which dust will adhere. Nor do dead plants require watering. Soaking or washing a basket is not a good idea – the plant fibres will swell and break. Water can also remove evidence of original use. A basket with historic berry stains speaks to us eloquently of both its beauty and utility.

Baskets do not benefit from repeated cleaning. Occasional vacuuming to remove surface dust is adequate. Secure an old nylon stocking or piece of nylon net over the end of the nozzle and use a soft artist's brush to sweep dust toward the vacuum.

Handle baskets carefully – damage and distortion are not easily repaired. Lift from the bottom – the edges and handles may not support the basket's weight. Crushed or flattened baskets can sometimes be gently reshaped in a humid room (such as a bathroom). Over a period of time, ease out the shape with pads of tissue paper. Coiled baskets can sometimes be held together with thread. But it is a good idea to consult a conservator before attempting repairs.

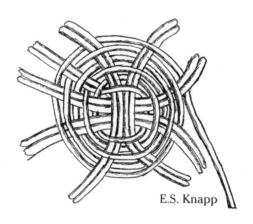

E.S. Knapp

Should Auld Furniture Be Forgot?

Well, the party's over. But how well has the furniture survived?

Pushing the table into the corner and pulling out the musical chairs did put some strain on the joints – the furniture's. In future, we'll carry them and, in the meantime, repair the damage. Uncle Harry's lunge unbalanced the last free chair, and it could warp permanently if not straightened now. White glue will do the job, after the joints are cleaned. And while we've got the glue out, we can stick down the loose inlay that caught Aunt Bea's boa. An empty bottle might do for a weight until it dries, with waxed paper to isolate it from any excess glue.

It's also time to move that table away from the window. Solar radiation will discolour the wood and damage the finish. The heat will cause the wood to dry out, too. Like partying relatives, wooden furnishings are sensitive to available moisture. If it's too dry, wood shrinks and cracks ... too much humidity, and it swells and may become warped. Potted plants should also be moved off the sideboard. Misting the leaves creates a humid micro-environment, and there's always the danger of a spill when watering. Luckily, the vase on the piano hasn't leaked yet (not that a waterproof mat underneath would have helped when Max started tossing roses at Cousin Louisa).

Despite all the coasters, a few cups were left for auld lang syne. We'll try a little boiled linseed oil rubbed into the white ring, vigorously wiping off the excess, which will darken without ever losing its stickiness. For the water marks on furniture with a shellac finish (e.g., French polish), dampen a cloth with denatured alcohol and rub in the direction of the grain. Of course, we'll practise on an obscure corner before tackling the tabletop.

Everything else will need a good dusting. Perhaps this is the year to resolve to hem the dust cloths – loose veneer is so easily snagged by ragged rags. And while the feather duster did make a lovely hat for Aunt Dolores, it's not suitable for dusting furniture – the spines can break and scratch the finish. The patina of a well-used antique is of aesthetic and historic value, like the laugh-lines on an aged aunt. Valuable heirlooms should be merely wiped with a slightly dampened cloth.

But those old chairs Freddy unearthed would benefit from a pick-me-up. Second-hand furniture can be cleaned with a 40:1 mixture of warm water and vinegar, or warm water and ammonia. Wipe it on with a damp cloth and quickly dry with a clean cloth. Sticky old wax can hold dust in corners; it can be removed with a little mineral spirits.

Before the next celebration begins, we should think about waxing those pieces that receive a lot of use. But we will abandon the excesses of the past – no more silicone-based sprays, lemon oil and other oils that interact with existing finishes. A little clear paste wax will enhance the shine of an already polished surface while providing some protection against scratches and moisture. Apply as thin a coat as possible, and polish well with a soft cloth. We won't overdo it, though. Three or four times a year is enough partying for any old furniture.

Moby Dick's Legacy

T here is much to see in a movie besides the actors. Watch closely the old classic *Moby Dick* and you'll see the whale teeth used as belaying pins along the bulwarks of the *Pequod*. Whale hunters used as much as they could of the sea mammal's carcass. The meat and blubber are long gone, but the teeth, bones and baleen of Moby Dick's relatives live on in artifacts.

Although bones and teeth are chemically similar, their physical structure reflects their different functions and enables us to identify them. Like elephant and walrus tusks, a whale's teeth are made of ivory, dense, white and hard. Ivory is finely grained and can be carved with little preparation. Whales' teeth became a popular medium for scrimshaw, decorative carvings done on ivory, bone or shell, especially by sailors on long voyages. Besides scrimshaw, ivory has been fashioned into intricate carvings and jewellery.

The bones of whales, much more abundant than the teeth, have been even more widely used. From a bone's marrow radiate tiny blood vessels. When bone is carved into buttons and cutlery handles, these vessels mark the surface with tiny dark spots and pits. A whale's mandible (jawbone) is whiter and denser than its other bones – fine enough to be carved into miniature models, strong enough for Captain Ahab's peg-leg.

Inuit model ship made of walrus tusk, bone and, perhaps, baleen (Joanne Boyer, RBCM 8933).

Whalebone also refers to baleen, which is not a bone at all. Like the horns of cattle and rhinos, baleen is a protein similar to hair and fingernails. Baleen whales, such as the Blue, Humpback and Grey, have large sheets of it in their mouths, which they use to filter the plankton and other small organisms that they eat. It is easy to cut and shape. In a pre-plastic age, baleen found many uses where a lightweight, flexible, water-resistant material was needed. Manufacturers in the early 19th century used it for the struts of umbrellas and parasols; it was the perfect material for "boning" corsets.

Vegetable ivory and French Ivory are neither ivory nor bone. Some palms, especially the Ivory Palm of the Andean plains, produce a dense, hard, white nut that can be cut and carved. French Ivory is a marketing name for celluloid, a plastic widely used in the 1920s and '30s (see Plastics Forever?, page 46).

Both bone and ivory are absorbent. Coloured storage materials can stain them, as can sulphur-containing substances such as rubber or wool. Oils absorbed from handling contribute to a tendency to yellow with age. After many years, bone and ivory develop a natural yellowish-brown patina that should be preserved.

After their removal from their damp origins in mouth and flesh, teeth, baleen and bones are susceptible to changes in humidity. Heat or dryness will cause them to crack and split; but once acclimatized, these artifacts will warp and split if they get wet. Keep them out of direct sunlight and away from the heat of fireplace or spotlight. A light dusting with a soft brush is the safest method of cleaning, though sometimes surface soil can be removed with a barely dampened swab.

The great shroud of the sea rolls still over the bones of Moby Dick and Captain Ahab, but the great white artifacts are ours to treasure.

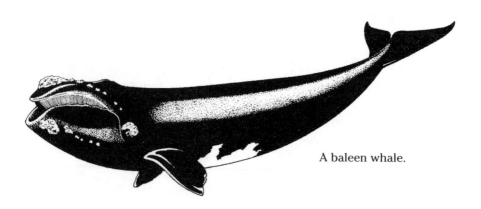

A baleen whale.

Fossil Futures

Rocking around the quarry, you stumble on a fossil. Can you dig it? It depends. Are you on private or Crown land? Do you have permission? Although you can pick up loose fossils from the surface of Crown lands, excavation in B.C. requires a permit.

Before you roll those boulders ... do you have your notebook and pencil handy? Unless the exact location and stratigraphic position is recorded, your fossil will be only a curiosity with no scientific interest or value. A map will help you pinpoint the location; a camera will assist in documentation. Make a waterproof label, including the date and the names of those present when the fossil was collected, and tie it to the specimen – adhesives can cause complications later. If the fossil is in pieces, make a careful sketch labelling the parts, so that it is possible to reassemble it later. Wrap your finds temporarily in newspaper or cloth and label the outside of the wrappings.

Inform your local museum or university about what you have found. They will be interested in recording your finds and can provide contacts for the local palaeontology society and information on preservation.

Preservation, you say? These things have been rock-steady for millions of years! Unfortunately, careless packaging and rough handling can qualify *you* as an erosion factor. Store your fossil on a bed of polyethylene foam in its own box. Use tissue between the stone and the foam – batting can catch and pull off fragments. Put a lid on the box to protect the fossil from dust; wrapping and rewrapping it in paper or plastic amounts to unnecessary handling. If your find includes bone that is not completely fossilized, the remaining calcium carbonate could be eroded by the acids in wood and ordinary cardboard. Get your rocks off the shelf and into polyethylene or acrylic boxes and acid-free tissue.

Wet finds should be dried very slowly. Wrap them in clear polyethylene. A few slits in the plastic will allow evaporation at a slow rate. But if your specimens begin to crack or grow mould, close the slits and seek expert advice.

Fossilized material that is already dry can be damaged by the addition of moisture. Dry bone can swell and crack. If the fossil contains pyrite – an iron oxide recognizable by its rust colour – moisture can initiate *pyrite disease*, active oxidation that is very difficult to stop. Store these fossils in a sealed container with conditioned silica gel to keep the relative humidity below 40 per cent.

Mammoth molar, 10,000 to 20,000 years old (D. Gillan, RBCM.EH1994.003.0051).

Seek advice before trying to clean up your fossils – the silt and clay around them can contain significant clues. Even if your hand is as steady as a rock, inexpert scratching and grinding can obliterate a record that has stood the test of 100 million years.

Art and the Rainforest

They were bleached to a pinkish silver colour and cracked by the sun, but nothing could make them mean or poor....

Fallen mortuary pole, Q'una, 1972 (Alan Hoover, RBCM PN7619-B).

So wrote Emily Carr in *Klee Wyck*, of the poles at Q'una (Skedans) that inspired some of her most famous paintings.

An old pole in an old place is a sombre sight, but those being carved today will not meet the same fate, mouldering away in abandoned communities.

Nineteenth-century poles were set deep in rock-lined holes, and fell in 50 to 100 years. The same rainfall that permits the growth of huge trees facilitates their decay. Entering at ground level or through areas of end-grain, the water supports insects, fungi and bacteria. Decaying wood in turn supports new plant growth.

New poles are no longer set in the ground. They are suspended from a metal support attached to the back with room at the bottom for air to circulate. Some of the poles in Thunderbird Park at the RBCM have metal caps to protect the exposed end-grain from our 650 mm (25 in) of annual rainfall, and there are plans to cap the others. Trees and bushes are kept at a distance to promote air

107

circulation and avoid dripping water. In the past, old poles have been brought to museums for preservation. These are kept indoors, where they have been allowed to dry completely and are no longer at risk of decay.

Traditionally, poles were highlighted with colour, but coating an outdoor wooden sculpture with paint or varnish can cause more problems than it solves. The coating protects only as long as the surface is unbroken. Flaking paint can carry away weathered wood and allow moisture to become trapped inside the sculpture, leading to rapid fungal growth. Water-repellent preservatives – mixtures of solvent, wax and biocide – that are used on construction lumber can provide some protection for old wood, but shelter from rain is more effective.

To see the only traditional Northwest Coast village site with standing totem and mortuary poles means a trip to the traditional Haida village, Sgan gwaay, on Anthony Island. There, conservators from the RBCM have helped devise and implement a maintenance plan to preserve the poles *in situ*.

Otherwise, let your imagination take you to Q'una (Skedans village) as George Dawson photographed it in 1878 – the model of the village on the third floor of the Royal B.C. Museum preserves our contact with that lost community in a way that conservators never can.

Pack Up All Your Cares

If the care of your heritage is getting you down, it may be time to pack it off to your deserving kin. But plan ahead so the treasures arrive intact – packing for transit is different than packing for storage.

A sealed plastic bag will isolate the artifact from pollutants in the packing materials, from travelling pests and jam – should you be unwise enough to send heritage preserves in the same parcel. The bag will ensure that the artifact arrives with the same level of humidity with which it left, and, should the worst occur, keep all the broken pieces together. If the artifact has a very fragile surface, however, wrap it in acid-free tissue first; polyethylene can develop enough static electricity to lift off fibres and fragments.

Unless you are bequeathing Aunt Maude's embroidered pillows, cushioning the item is necessary. Materials of dubious stability can be used because the packaging is temporary. Consider the weight of the artifact and that the cushioning material must repeat its performance. Crumpled tissue will bounce back if packed around a very light object, but will be flattened by a marble bust. Styrofoam is only good for a single impact – once dented, it stays that way. Polyester quilt batting is an excellent cushioning material, but should never be used directly against an artifact – the fibres will cling to any rough surface and pull off fragments when removed.

Polyethylene foam, polyurethane foam, bubble pack, even popcorn (yes, real popcorn – air-popped, not pre-buttered!) will distribute the force of impact, but they can become compressed with time, excessive load or high temperatures. Consider that larger packages tend to be dropped more on their bottoms; smaller, lighter objects tend to be dropped from greater heights. It is possible to calculate both the type and amount of cushioning required. When you decide who deserves the glass harmonicon✛, seek expert advice.

The size of the artifact and the choice of carrier will determine the crate. A small item in a cardboard box can be safely carried by hand; the same box would be less satisfactory for mailing Uncle Frank's collection of cannon balls. A wooden crate will provide protection and reduce damage from handling. Aunt Nellie's penny-farthing bicycle will be awkward to pack, but secure in a crate it will probably suffer less than she did in her final road race. If you have a collection of items, make sure

---

✛ *The name* Harmonicon *was first given to a series of musical glasses of graded size, the tones being produced by running wet fingers around the rims of the glasses. An early model of this instrument survives in the Horniman Museum in London…. Efforts to combine the Harmonicon with a keyboard produced an instrument with the glasses arranged in two rows and sounded by a series of levers, but no picture can be found of this German instrument of 1784, played for Frances Barkley in Brazil in 1787.* – from *The Remarkable World of Frances Barkley:1769–1845* by Beth Hill (Gray's Publishing, 1978)

they are compatible travelling companions – Grandpa's anvil should not accompany Grandma's china dogs.

Although FRAGILE and HANDLE WITH CARE labels are ineffectual, clear and consistent labelling will help ensure your parcel's prompt arrival. If you are re-using a container, be sure to remove all the old labels. Dress your package for success: Cousin Louis may value his inheritance more if it comes in an impressive box. And don't forget to include an inventory – you don't want the pearls to be composted with the popcorn!

The Times in a Capsule

The clock is approaching midnight. Are you thinking of capturing this moment for posterity? Perhaps you want to create a time capsule to hold the essence of today's life for the edification and delight of future generations. If so, time is ticking away – there is planning to do if both the container and its contents are to withstand the passage of years.

As the clock is striking ONE, *your capsule will be fair begun ...* if you start with stainless steel. Little is known about the very long-term stability of plastics, although polyethylene that can be sealed may be suitable for indoor storage. For burial or enclosure in a wall, a stainless-steel container should be used and welded shut, with instructions about opening it marked clearly on the outside.

The clock chimes TWO, *time to think about the dew ...* and frost and ground water level. Choose a protected location as the capsule's storage chamber, and line it with fibreglass insulation to protect the contents from radical temperature changes. Plastic will probably crack if exposed to repeated freezing. The chamber should also protect the capsule from excess weight.

The clock is striking THREE, *dryness means longevity* ... so plan on packing one-fifth of the capsule with dried silica gel crystals. Seal the crystals in a cotton or linen bag and leave them overnight in a 150°C (300°F) oven to drive off all moisture. Add the silica gel last, just before sealing the capsule.

The clock ticks on and strikes again, at FOUR *remove all oxygen* ... for the greatest security against decay. Flush the capsule with nitrogen for 15 minutes before sealing.

Now the clock is striking FIVE, *time to think of what's inside!* Mass-produced papers, rubber, plastic, paints and varnishes are acidic and will become even more so when sealed in the micro-climate of the capsule. If items of dubious stability are included, seal them in polyethylene or Mylar to minimize their effect on the rest of the contents. Consider that many things are already being kept in museums and archives by people who make preservation their daily work. Newspapers, for instance, will probably be better preserved on microfiche than in a time capsule.

Time draws on, the clock strikes SIX; *reconsider any pix* ... or snapshots. Photographs are known to be unstable unless printed in black-and-white on archival-standard paper. Magnetically recorded material – audio and video tape – deteriorates in quality unless rewound periodically. Consider, too, that there may be difficulty locating outdated playing devices in the future.

As the clock is chiming SEVEN, *turn your thought toward the heavens* ... and consider solar-powered batteries. Otherwise, remove the batteries from any electronic devices, and include a note detailing the voltage and current requirements.

It's getting late, it's striking EIGHT, *metals will have a surer fate* ... if they are neither polished nor coated. Degrease them with acetone and handle them with white cotton gloves (unless you want to have your fingerprints preserved as well).

Now the clock is striking NINE, *rejoice that you still have some time* ... to consider all these difficulties, time to make insightful and imaginative choices, time to make all this effort worthwhile.

Ten, eleven ... It's a big responsibility, describing a culture by its material goods. It is the job curators do, selecting those *defining objects*, those artifacts of curiosity and delight, the rare and the representative that make the Royal B.C. Museum's collection our province's time capsule. Museum conservators ensure that those collections will still be there for the next millennium. And the one after that.

Consulting a Conservator

T he best place to find a conservator is at a museum. If you have questions about preserving a treasured heirloom, contact the conservation department of your local (or nearest) museum. Conservators close to home will have intimate knowledge of the local environment, which may affect the object in question.

G. Luxton, RBCM

In British Columbia, you can contact the Conservation Department of the Royal B.C. Museum:

675 Belleville Street
Victoria, B.C.
V8W 9W2

phone: 250-387-3647
e-mail: vthorp@royalbcmuseum.bc.ca
web site: www.royalbcmuseum.bc.ca

Outside B.C., if your local museum or art gallery can't help you, contact the Canadian Association for the Conservation of Cultural Property (CAC):

400 - 280 Metcalfe
Ottawa, Ontario
K2P 1R7

```
phone:      613-567-0099
fax:        613-233-5438
e-mail:     smarion@museums.ca
web site:   www.cac-accr.ca
```

or the Canadian Conservation Institute
```
            1030 Innes Road
            Ottawa, Ontario
            K1A 0M5
phone:      613-991-5701
```

Suggested Reading

Canadian Conservation Institute. 1996. *CCI Notes*. Ottawa: Canadian Conservation Institute.

Clapp, Anne F. 1987. *Curatorial Care of Works of Art on Paper*. New York: Nick Lyons Books.

Finch, Karen, and Greta Putnam. 1985. *The Care and Preservation of Textiles*. London: B.T. Batsford.

Florian, Mary-Lou E., Dale Paul Kronkright and Ruth E. Norton. 1990. *The Conservation of Artifacts Made From Plant Materials*. Princeton, N.J.: Princeton University Press.

Grattan, David W., editor. 1993. *Saving the Twentieth Century: The Conservation of Modern Materials*. Ottawa: Canadian Conservation Institute.

Mailand, Harold F. 1980. *Considerations for The Care of Textiles and Costumes*. Indianapolis, Minnesota: Indianapolis Museum of Art.

Ogden, Sherelyn, editor. 1994. *Preservation of Library and Archival Materials: A Manual* rev. ed. Andover, Massachusetts: Northeast Document Conservation Centre.

Stout, George L. 1975. *The Care of Pictures*. New York: Dover Publications.

Acknowledgements

I am a trained conservator of textiles – I don't really know very much about other materials. Without the help of my colleagues at the Royal British Columbia Museum, this work would not have been possible. Conservators Kjerstin Mackie, Lisa Bengston, George Field and, especially, Val Thorp suggested topics, found (and explained) scholarly articles and books, read and criticized drafts. They also did my job while I chewed my nails over some unmanageable phrase and humoured me when I subjected them to stupid puns. Natural History Collections Managers Joan Kerik and John Pinder-Moss gave me advice about fossils and plants, and Mike McNall supplied information on firearms. Betty Walsh, Conservator at BC Archives held my hand through the articles on paper, books and photographs.

Arlene Yaworsky was the editor of *Discovery* when these articles originally appeared in its pages. With great patience and enthusiasm she steered me in the direction of comprehensibility. She suggested topics which I ignored, helped track down the illustrations I was too lazy to find and argued me into becoming a better writer; ultimately, she agitated for the publication of this book. If you enjoy these articles, thank Arlene Yaworsky. If you find any mistakes, blame me.

Colleen Wilson

All articles in this book were originally published in *Discovery*, the news and events magazine of the Friends of the Royal B.C. Museum, from April 1995 to July 2002, mostly in Colleen Wilson's column, "Conservator's Corner". Most of the originals were edited by Arlene Yaworsky, a few by Gerry Truscott. The versions that appear in this book were modified a little by the author, then edited a little more by Gerry Truscott, with help from Candace Kinnee and Bob Ashforth.

Designed and typeset by Gerry Truscott, RBCM.
   The type is Cheltenham Book.
Cover designed by Chris Tyrrell, RBCM.
All illustrations are from copyright-free sources, except
   for those belonging to the Royal B.C. Museum
   (marked "RBCM").

Printed and bound in Canada by Kromar Printing.

Index

Page numbers in **bold**
indicate the main entry.

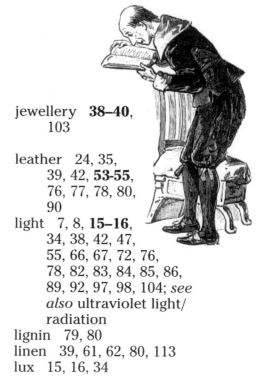

124